Table of Contents

Keeping up With the Dinosaurs 3
Nippers, Rippers, and Grinders 4
Get a Clue! 5
Lumps, Bumps, and Scars 6
Fossils 7
Scales, Feathers, Hair 8
One Happy Community 9
From Egg to Tadpole to Frog 10
Toadly Froggin' Around 11
Secret Code for Worm Lovers 12
Hibernation 13
Endangered Animals 14
Feathered Friend Feeders 15
Going Places 16
Six-Legged Friends 15
Insects in Winter 16
Ants in Your Pants! 19
Body Building Blocks 20
Build a Blood Cell! 21
Framework 22
Your Pizza's Path 23
Breathing Tree 24
Your Body's Pipeline 25
Lub-Dub, Lub-Dub 26
Think Tank 27
Your Body's Messenger Service 28
You Are What You Eat 29
Tasty Plant Parts 30
Plant Parts 31
Slurp, Slurp 32
Tree-mendous Plant 33
Leaves or Needles 34
How Does Your Garden Grow? 35
Cruising Coconuts 36
The Solar System 37
Spinning Top 38
Space Shadows 39
How Big? 40
Mercury 41
Venus 42

Mars	43
Jupiter	44
Saturn	45
The Large Planets	46
Uranus	47
Neptune	48
The Twin Planets	49
Pluto	50
Read My Mind	51
The Milky Way Galaxy	52
Weight and Gravity	53
"Live Via Satellite"	54
Rain in the Rainforest	55
Lightning	56
A Funnel Cloud – Danger	57
Can You Pour Air?	58
Cool Color	59
The Invisible Force	60
Out of This World	61
Voom!	62
Magnets	63
Push and Pull	64
Machines of Old	65
Around and Around	66
Gearing Up	67
Ramps, Hills, and Slopes	68
Special Inclined Plane – Wedge	69
Simple + Simple = Compound	70
Work Savers	71
Answer Key	72–80

Frank Schaffer Publications®

Printed in the United States of America. All rights reserved. Limited Reproduction Permission: Permission to duplicate these materials is limited to the person for whom they are purchased. Reproduction for an entire school or school district is unlawful and strictly prohibited. Frank Schaffer Publications is an imprint of School Specialty Publishing. Copyright © 2006 School Specialty Publishing.

Send all inquiries to:
Frank Schaffer Publications
3195 Wilson Drive NW
Grand Rapids, Michigan 49534

Science—Grade 3

ISBN 0-7696-4943-2

1 2 3 4 5 6 7 8 9 10 WAL 10 09 08 07 06

Dinosaurs   Name _____

Keeping up With the Dinosaurs

Directions: Read the dinosaur facts below. Then, write true or false in the blanks before the sentences at the bottom of the page.

Paleontologists believe that the first true **dinosaurs** evolved on Earth about 225 million years ago and became extinct, or disappeared, about 65 million years ago. All true dinosaurs were land-living creatures. The gigantic prehistoric sea creatures, such as ichthyosaurs, mosasaurs and plesiosaurs, were not really dinosaurs. Pterosaurs were not really dinosaurs either. They were flying reptiles that looked like lizards with wings.

The word dinosaur means "terrible lizard," but dinosaurs were not lizards. Modern science now links dinosaurs to **birds**. Today's birds are thought to be the closest relatives to the dinosaurs. Crocodiles are also thought to be more distant relatives of the dinosaurs. Scientists believe all animals and plants living on Earth today are descendants of creatures that lived when dinosaurs roamed the earth.

True or false?

1. ___ The first dinosaurs evolved on Earth about 65 million years ago.

2. ___ Ichthyosaurs were true dinosaurs.

3. ___ Dinosaurs were not lizards.

4. ___ Scientists believe birds are related to dinosaurs.

5. ___ Some dinosaurs were flying reptiles.

Challenge:
Think of your favorite bird. List some ways this bird is like, or similar to, a dinosaur.

_____

_____

Dinosaurs Name_____

Nippers, Rippers, and Grinders

 1.  2.  3.

Scientists tell us that some dinosaurs were meat-eaters and others were plant-eaters. But how do the scientists know? By looking at the teeth of certain dinosaur fossils, scientists can tell what those dinosaurs ate. Meat-eaters had sharp, saw-edged teeth **(figure 1)** for cutting and ripping flesh. Plant-eating dinosaurs had either peg-like teeth **(figure 2)** for nipping plants or flat grinding teeth **(figure 3)** to munch tough twigs or leaves.

Directions:
1. Look at the kind of teeth of each dinosaur below.
2. Circle either "M" for meat-eater or "P" for plant-eater.

Meat-eater or Plant-eater

Tyrannosaurus
(tie-ran-o-SAWR-us) M   P

Parasaurolophus
(par-us-sawr-uh-LOW-fus) M   P

Monoclonius
(mah-no-KLONE-ee-us) M   P

Hypsilophodon
(HIP-sil-ahf-oh-don) M   P

Triceratops
(try-SAIR-uh-tops) M   P

Fantastic Fact
The **Tyrannosaurus**, whose name means "king of the tyrant lizards," was the largest meat-eater. It weighed over 8 tons and was over 50 feet long. Its teeth were over 6 inches long and had edges like a steak knife.

Dinosaurs

Name _____

Get a Clue!

Directions: Read the 16 clues below about a certain dinosaur. Use a science book or other resource materials and your own logical thinking to guess the name of the dinosaur. When you are finished, write your own clues about another dinosaur. Give it to someone else to see if he/she can guess the answer.

I am a dinosaur.

1. My name means "three-horned face."
2. My skull was 7 or 8 feet long.
3. I had a beaked mouth like a parrot.
4. I ate plants.
5. I walked on all four legs.
6. I was 30 feet long.
7. I weighed up to 10 tons.
8. I was one of the last dinosaurs to live.
9. I had 3 claws on my front feet.
10. I lived in Canada and the U.S.
11. I had a thick neck frill.
12. I had 3 horns on my skull.
13. I am the best-known horned dinosaur.
14. I used my horns for protection.
15. I had a small hoof on each toe.
16. I was named by O.C. Marsh in 1889.

I am a _____.

I am a dinosaur.

1. _____
2. _____
3. _____
4. _____
5. _____
6. _____
7. _____
8. _____
9. _____
10. _____

I am a _____.

Dinosaurs   Name _____

Lumps, Bumps and Scars

It's exciting when a **paleontologist** (a scientist who studies fossils) finds a dinosaur fossil. The fossil might be from a dinosaur no one has ever discovered before.

It might take years for paleontologists to put together most of a dinosaur's bones. The lumps, bumps and scars on the bones give them clues as to what the dinosaur might have looked like. These marks on the bones show where muscles were attached. By looking at the whole skeleton and the lumps, bumps and scars on each bone, paleontologists can guess the shape of the dinosaur's body.

Directions: The two skeletons below are make-believe dinosaurs that nobody has ever found. Study the skeletons. Use colored pencils, crayons or markers to draw right over the skeleton to show what these dinosaurs might have looked like. Then, name your dinosaurs.

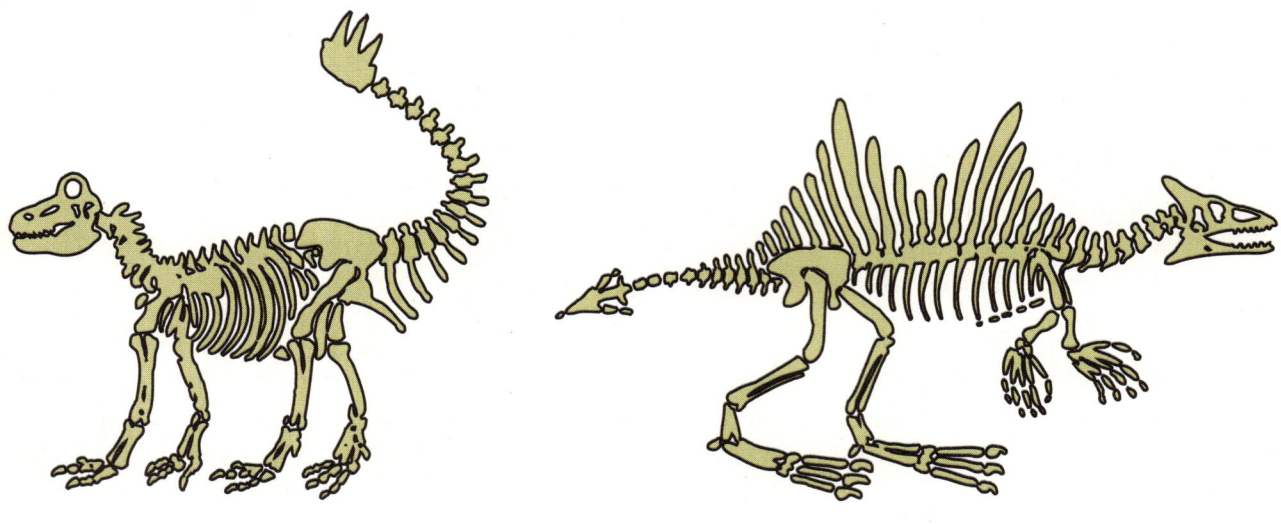

_____   _____

Fantastic Fact
Not all dinosaurs were huge giants. The **Compsognathus** (komp-SAHG-nay-thus) was the smallest dinosaur. It was about the same size as a crow, and it could run very fast.

Dinosaurs

Name _____

Fossils

Besides bone fossils, scientists have found other kinds of fossils. Below are the pictures of some of these other kinds of fossils.

Directions: Draw a line from the description of the kind of fossil to its picture.

- A dinosaur makes footprints in the soft mud. The mud hardens and turns into rock.

- Sometimes the skin of a dinosaur is changed into a fossil.

- The eggs of some dinosaurs have been changed into fossil eggs.

Directions: Carefully study these dinosaur footprints. Draw a line from the dinosaur to its footprints.

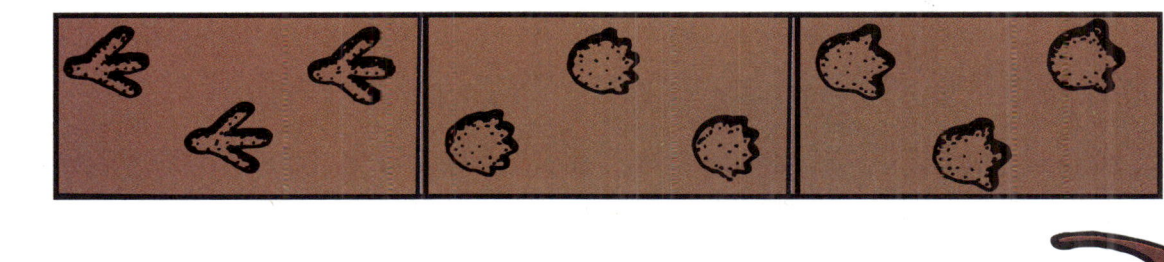

Triceratops

Megalosaurus

Parasaurolophus

Fantastic Fact
Fossil eggs of the **Protoceratops** (pro-toe-SAIR-uh-tops) have been found with the skeletons of tiny baby Protoceratops inside!

Animals, Birds, Insects

Name _____

Scales, Feathers, Hair

Directions:

Before this activity, collect pictures of animals. Examine the exterior, or the outside, of your animals. Write down two or more observations regarding the outside of your animals (for example, the birds are colorful, the puppies are furry, the snakes don't look that slimy, etc.). Share your observations.

Directions:

Categorize your pictures into three groups by looking at what is on the exterior of your animals. How did you decide which animals would be grouped together? On paper, create three columns. Title one **"Fish,"** one **"Birds"** and one **"Mammals"** and glue pictures under the specific category listed.

Glue each animal under the proper category. When the supply of pictures has been exhausted, make generalizations about the coverings of animals (for example, if an animal has feathers, it is a bird). You **CAN** judge an animal by its cover!

Animals, Birds, Insects

Name _____

One Happy Community

Most animals are more comfortable living with certain other animals and plants. This special group is called a **community**.

There are many kinds of communities. Some animals live in a forest community or a pond community. Others live in a desert, seashore or grassland community.

Directions: Look at the communities below and list five animals in each.

Pond Community   **Forest Community**

_____   _____
_____   _____
_____   _____
_____   _____
_____   _____

1. Why do you think these animals live together in the pond community?
   _____

2. Why do you think these animals live together in the forest community?
   _____

3. Some animals may live in more than one kind of a community. Name some animals that live in both a pond and forest community. _____
   _____

Investigate
Your backyard can be an animal community. Make a list of the animals that visit or live in your backyard. Don't forget those tiny ones you can't easily see.

Animals, Birds, Insects

Name _____

From Egg to Tadpole to Frog

The poem below tells about the changes that occur in a frog's life cycle. In every line, there is one word that doesn't make sense. Find the correct word in the Word Bank below and write it in the puzzle. **Hint:** The correct word rhymes with it.

The Life Cycle of a Frog

There is jelly on the legs (13)
    To protect the entire match. (11)
It takes tree to twenty-five days (7 down)
    Until they're ready to catch. (5)

Out comes a pollihog (18)
    When the time is just bright. (8)
It breathes using hills (14)
    And its size is very light. (4)

It loses its long scale (9)
    After pegs begin to grow. (1)
Digestion and breathing strange (12)
    In a process fast and glow. (2)

What helps a frog to seethe (3)
    Is its thin and moist chin. (6 down)
It also uses rungs (15)
    To let the hair in. (10)

Some frogs can skim like a duck. (6 across)
    And some can mop like a rabbit. (16)
Others climb bees like a squirrel (7 across)
    Which may seem a bunny habit. (17)

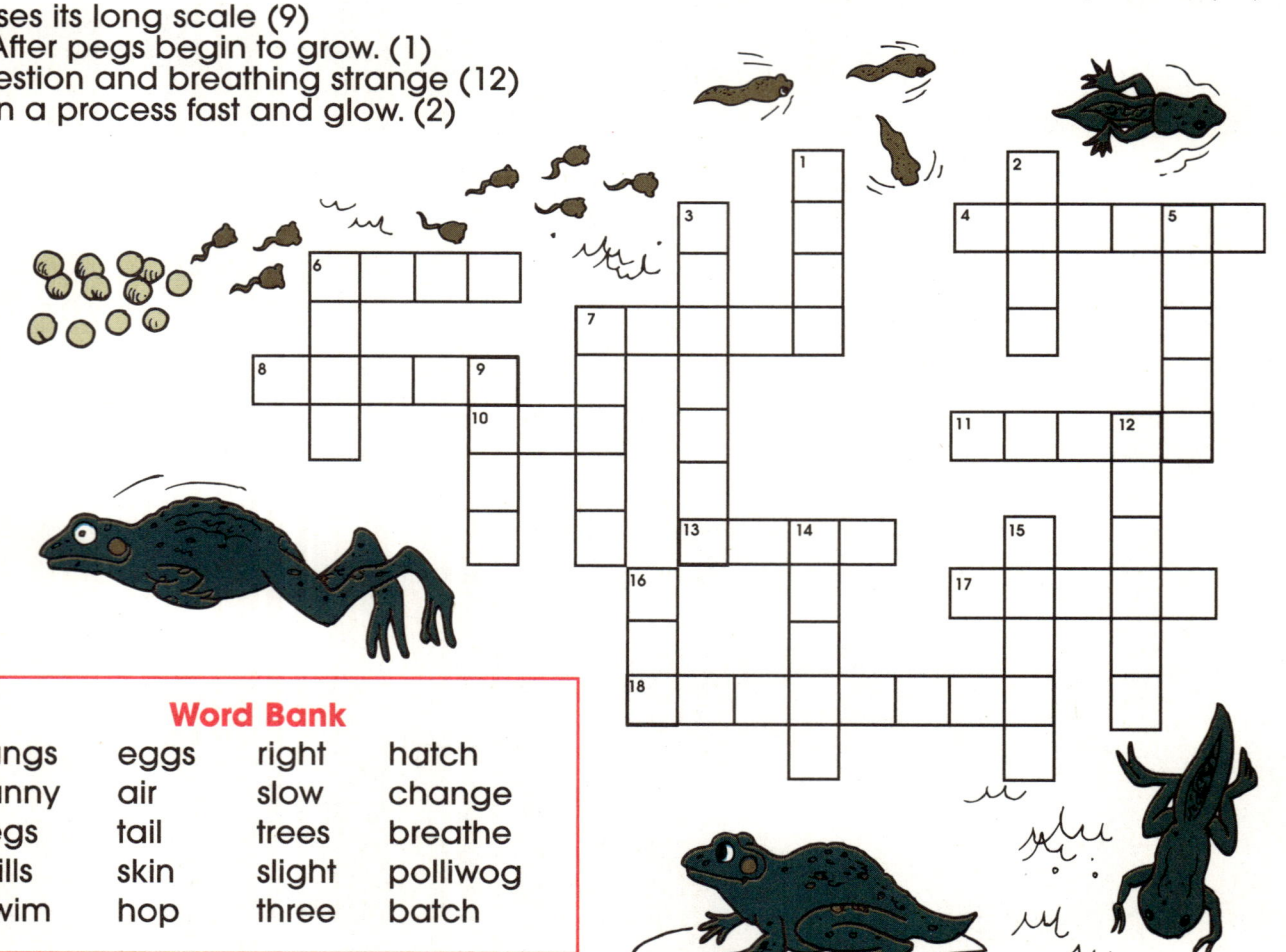

Word Bank

lungs	eggs	right	hatch
funny	air	slow	change
legs	tail	trees	breathe
gills	skin	slight	polliwog
swim	hop	three	batch

Published by Frank Schaffer Publications. Copyright protected.

Science: Grade 3

Animals, Birds, Insects

Name _____

Toadly Froggin' Around

Directions:
Read the information about frogs and toads.
Then, write **true** or **false** in front of each statement at the bottom.

Frogs and Toads

Both frogs and toads are amphibians. Amphibians spend part of their lives as water animals and part as land animals. In the early stages of their lives, amphibians breathe through gills, while as adults they develop lungs. Most amphibians lay eggs near water. Newly hatched frogs and toads both have tails that they later lose. Both often have poison glands in their skin to protect them from their enemies.

Frogs and toads are different in several ways. Most toads are broader, darker and flatter. Their skin is drier. Toads are usually covered with warts while frogs have smooth skin. Most toads live on land while most frogs prefer being in or near the water.

_____ 1. Both frogs and toads usually lay eggs near water.

_____ 2. Most frogs have drier skin than toads.

_____ 3. Very young amphibians breathe with lungs.

_____ 4. Frogs tend to be lighter in color.

_____ 5. An adult frog's tail helps support him while sitting.

_____ 6. Poison glands often protect frogs from an enemy.

_____ 7. A toad's skin is often bumpy.

_____ 8. Frogs and toads are both amphibians.

Animals, Birds, Insects   Name _____

Secret Code for Worm Lovers

Directions:

To decode the secret words, use the code below.

1. Earthworms can also be called __ __ __ __ __   __ __ __ __ __ __ __.
                                                    14 9 7 8 20   3 18 1 23 12 5 18 19

2. Earthworms have no __ __ __ __ or __ __ __ __.
                               5 1 18 19   5 25 5 19

3. Sections of an earthworm are called __ __ __ __ __ __ __ __.
                                               19 5 7 13 5 14 20 19

4. Earthworms __ __ __ __ __ __ __ through their __ __ __ __.
                     2 18 5 1 20 8 5   19 11 9 14

5. Earthworms eat __ __ __ __.
                     19 15 9 12

6. As they __ __ __ __ __ __ through the soil, they give plants the __ __ __
                2 21 18 18 15 23   1 9 18
   that they need.

Animals, Birds, Insects

Hibernation

Have you ever wondered why some animals hibernate? Some animals sleep all winter. This sleep is called **hibernation**.

Animals get their warmth and energy from food. Some animals cannot find enough food in the winter. They must eat large amounts of food in the autumn. Their bodies store this food as fat. Then, in winter, they hibernate. Their bodies live on the stored fat. Since their bodies need much less food during hibernation, they can stay alive without eating anymore food during the winter.

Some animals that hibernate are bats, chipmunks, bears, snakes and turtles.

Directions:

Match:

Animals that hibernate . . .
    eat and store food   in the winter.
    go to sleep   in the autumn.

Underline:

Hibernation . . .   is a sleep that some animals go into for the winter.
    is the time of year to gather food for the winter.

Circle Yes or No:

Animals get their warmth and energy from food.	Yes	No
Some animals cannot find enough food in the winter.	Yes	No
Animals hibernate because they are lazy.	Yes	No
Animals need less food while they are hibernating.	Yes	No

Color the animals that hibernate.

Animals, Birds, Insects

Name _____

Endangered Animals

You will never see a dodo bird or a saber-tooth tiger. These animals are gone forever. They are *extinct*.

The animals on this page are not extinct, but they are in danger of becoming extinct. They are *endangered*. There may not be enough of them to reproduce.

There are many reasons why some animals are endangered. The signs on this page give clues to three main reasons.

Look at the signs. What do you think the three reasons are? Write them below.

1. _____
_____
2. _____
_____
3. _____

Directions: Unscramble the names of these endangered animals.

| dalb gleae | nereg teltur | lueb laweh | bremit lofw |

_____ _____ _____ _____

Investigate
There are more than 100 endangered animals in North America. Find the name of one that lives near your area. Make a poster to help people become aware of this animal and the danger it is in.

Animals, Birds, Insects

Name _____

Feathered Friend Feeders

You will need: grapefruit halves, cereal, peanuts, birdseed, string or yarn, stale bread, peanut butter, plastic knives, cookie cutter shapes

Directions:

1. **Grazing Grapefruits**
Start with half of an empty grapefruit skin. (Clean this beforehand and share the fruit if you like.) Poke three holes in the skin and thread three pieces of string through the holes. Tie them together so the grapefruit will be balanced when it hangs. Fill the grapefruit skin with nuts, cereal or birdseed. Hang the bird feeders on a tree branch.

2. **Cookie Cutter Café**
Cut a shape out of a slice of stale bread using a cookie cutter. Then, spread one side of the bread with peanut butter and sprinkle nuts or seeds onto the peanut butter until the bread is well coated. Next, carefully poke a small hole through the center of the bread and thread a piece of yarn through it. Hang the bird feeder in a tree to create a yummy café for your feathered friends.

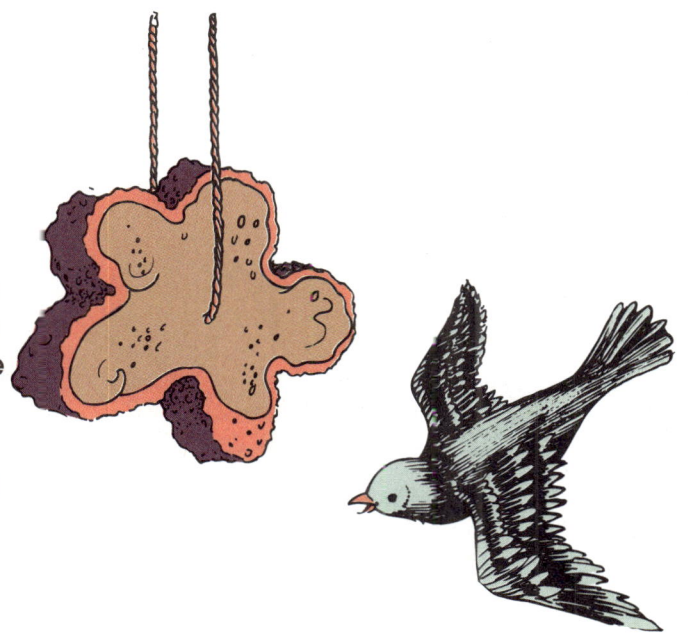

Note: Birds may become dependent on the feeder for their food supply. You should continue feeding the birds during the winter months when food may be scarce.

Animals, Birds, Insects

Name _____

Going Places

Looking at a bird's feet can tell you a lot about how they are used. Look at the birds' feet below. Unscramble each bird's name. Write the bird's name by the sentence that best describes it.

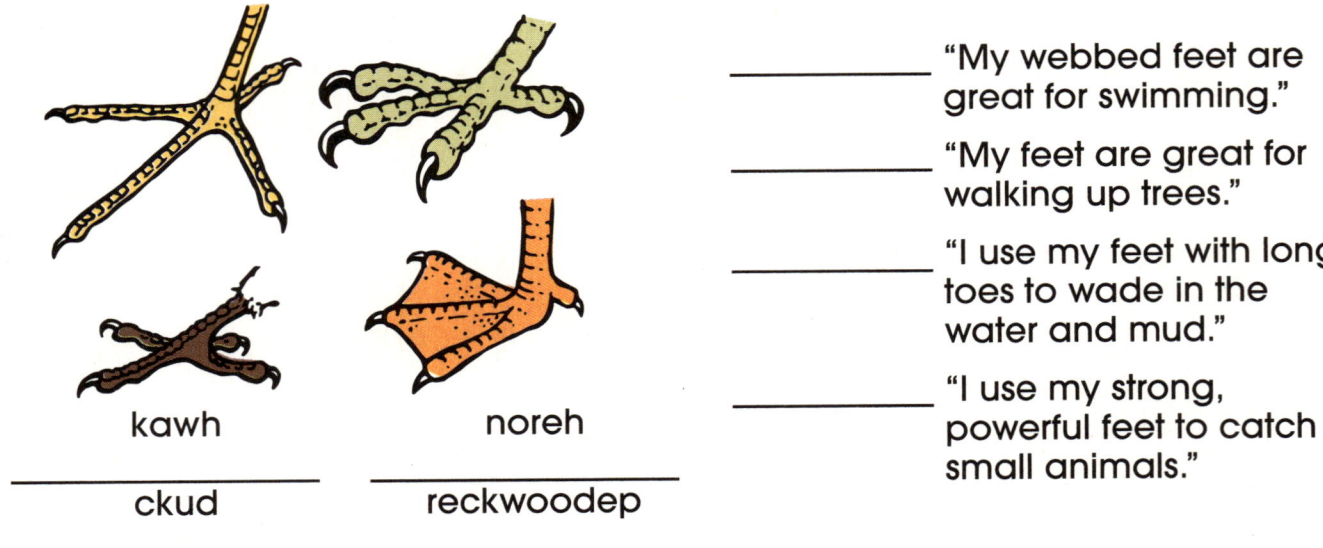

kawh

noreh

_____
ckud

_____
reckwoodep

_____ "My webbed feet are great for swimming."

_____ "My feet are great for walking up trees."

_____ "I use my feet with long toes to wade in the water and mud."

_____ "I use my strong, powerful feet to catch small animals."

Can the shape of a bird's bill tell you anything about what it eats? Look closely at the bills below. Unscramble each bird's name. Write the bird's name by the sentence that best describes it.

noreh

reckwoodep

_____
bumminghird

_____
kawh

_____
panicel

_____
dinalcar

_____ "I pound holes in wood to find insects."

_____ "I use my long bill to get nectar from flowers."

_____ "I use my strong bill to crack open seeds."

_____ "I use my sharp bill to tear the flesh of animals."

_____ "I stab at small fish with my sharp bill."

_____ "I scoop up large mouthfuls of water and fish."

Published by Frank Schaffer Publications. Copyright protected.

Science: Grade 3

Animals, Birds, Insects

Name _____

Six-Legged Friends

The largest group of animals belongs to the group called invertebrates—or animals without backbones. This large group is the **insect** group.

Insects are easy to tell apart from other animals. Adult insects have three body parts and six legs. The first body part is the **head**. On the head are the mouth, eyes and antennae. The second body part is the **thorax**. On it are the legs and wings. The third part is the **abdomen**. On it are small openings for breathing.

Directions: Color the body parts of the insect above: head-red, thorax-yellow, abdomen-blue.

Draw an insect below. Make your insect one-of-a-kind. Be sure it has the correct number of body parts, legs, wings and antennae. Fill in the information.

Insect's name _____   Warning _____

Length _____   _____

Where found _____   _____

Food _____   _____

Investigate
Many people think that spiders are insects. Spiders and insects are alike in many ways, but spiders are not insects. Find out how the two are different.

Animals, Birds, Insects

Name _____

Insects in Winter

In the summertime, insects can be seen buzzing and fluttering around us. But as winter's cold weather begins, suddenly the insects seem to disappear. Do you know where they go?

Many insects, such as flies and mosquitoes, find a warm place to spend the winter. They live in cellars, barns, attics, caves and tree holes.

Beetles and ants try to dig deep into the ground. Some beetles stack up in piles under rocks or dead leaves.

In the fall, female grasshoppers and crickets lay their eggs and die. The eggs hatch in the spring.

Bees also try to protect themselves from the winter cold. Honeybees gather in a ball in the middle of their hive. The bees stay in this tight ball trying to stay warm.

Winter is very hard for insects, but each spring the survivors come out and the buzzing and fluttering begins again.

Directions: Circle Yes or No.

In the winter, insects look for a warm place to live. Yes No

noise, such as buzzing, can be heard all winter long. Yes No

Some beetles and ants dig deep into the ground. Yes No

every insect finds a warm home for the winter. Yes No

Crickets and grasshoppers lay their eggs and die. Yes No

the honeybees gather in a ball in their hive. Yes No

Survivors of the cold weather come out each spring. Yes No

Animals, Birds, Insects

Name _____

Ants in Your Pants!

Ants are busy insects, always moving, always working hard. They live together in colonies, and every ant has a job to do to help the others. When someone cannot sit still and is wiggly and eager to get going, people sometimes ask, "Are there ants in your pants?"

You will need:

ink pad
construction paper
pen
crayons

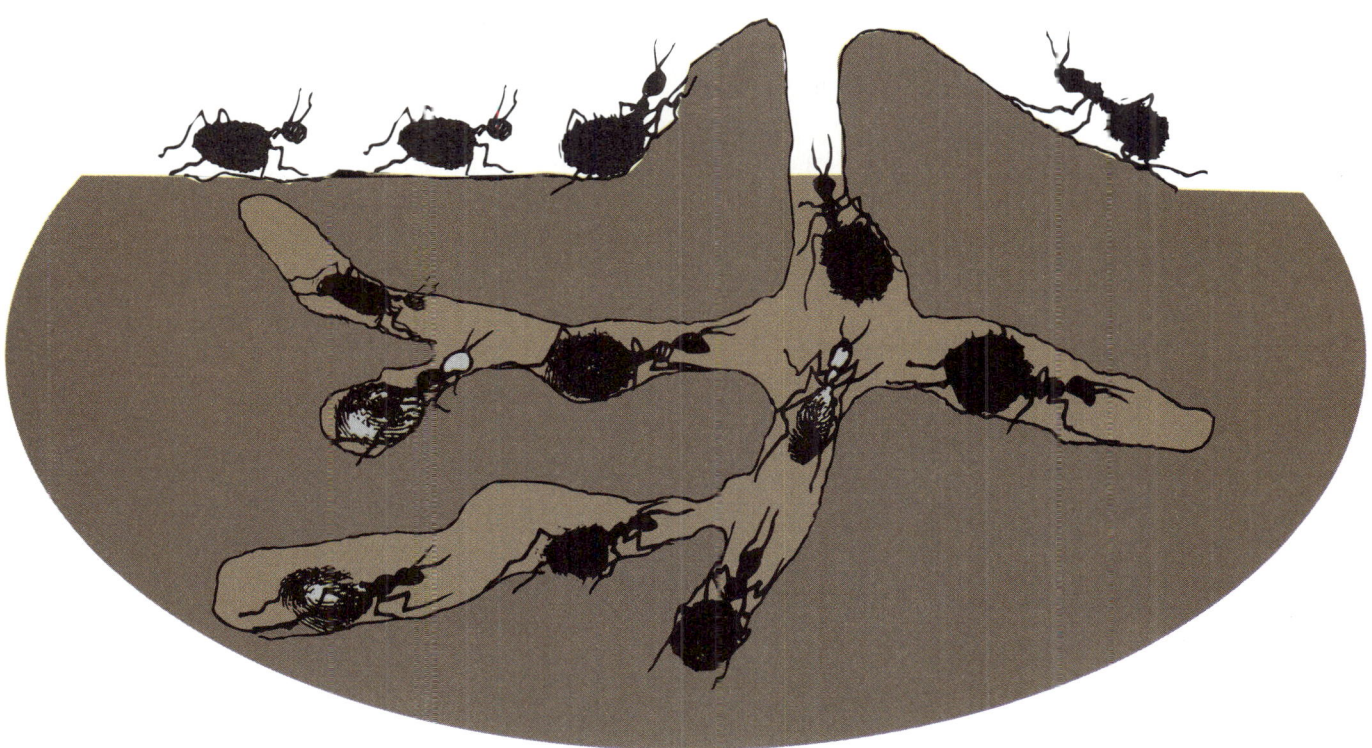

Directions: Create a drawing of an ant city. Begin by drawing a series of underground tunnels on a piece of construction paper. To create ants in their tunnels, press your fingertips onto an ink pad and then press your inky prints onto the paper. When the ink dries, you can use a pen to draw legs and antennae on the ants.

As an added touch, create a story about your busy ant community.

Human Body

Name _____

Body Building Blocks

Just like some houses are built with bricks, your body is built with cells. Every part of your body is made of cells.

Cells differ in **size** and **shape**, but they all have a few things in common. All cells have a nucleus. The **nucleus** is the center of the cell. It controls the cell's activities.

Cells can **divide** and become two cells exactly like the original cell.

Your body has many kinds of cells. Each kind has a special job. **Muscle** cells help you move. **Nerve** cells carry messages between your brain and other parts of your body. Blood cells carry **oxygen** to other cells in your body.

Directions:
Complete each sentence using the words in bold from above.

muscle cell

The _ _ _ _ _ _ _ controls the cell's activities.
    3

Cells differ in _ _ _ _ and _ _ _ _ _.
            2   1

One cell can _ _ _ _ _ _ into two cells.
               6

_ _ _ _ _ _ cells help you move.
   5

Blood cells carry _ _ _ _ _ _ to other cells in your body.
              4

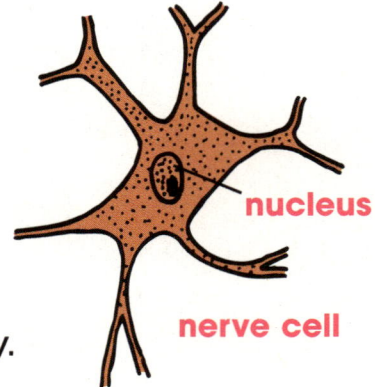
nucleus

nerve cell

Unscramble the numbered letters above to discover this amazing fact.

You began life as a _ _ _ _ _ _ cell!
             1 2 3 4 5 6

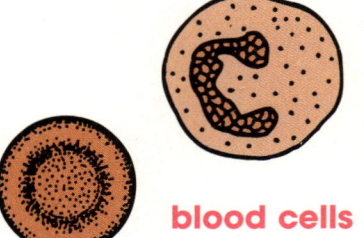
blood cells

Fantastic Fact
People and most animals are made of billions or even trillions of cells. But some animals are made of only one cell. To find out more about these animals, look up **protozoans** in your library.

Human Body

Build a Blood Cell!

Each blood cell has its own parts. Look at the picture below and study the parts of the red blood cells. Remember, this is much bigger than a real cell.

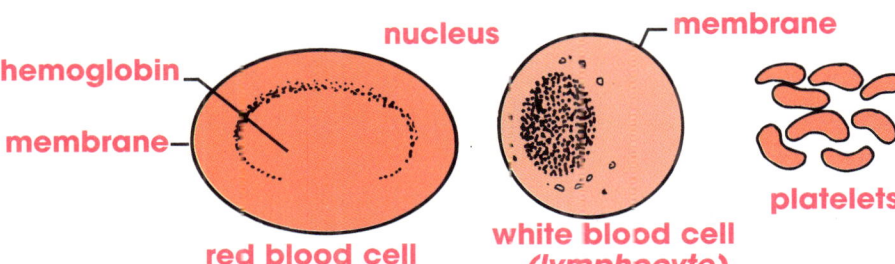

You will need:

1 plastic bag that seals
1 dark button
½ cup prepared red gelatin

Directions:

1. Put the gelatin in the bag.
2. Place the button in the bag.
3. Squeeze the button to the center of the bag.

Draw your red blood cell and label its parts.

Human Body

Name _____

Framework

What gives you your **shape**? Like a house's frame, your body also has a frame. It is called your **skeleton**. Your skeleton is made of more than two hundred bones.

Your skeleton helps your body move. It does this by giving your **muscles** a place to attach. Your skeleton also **protects** the soft organs inside your body from injury.

Bones have a hard, outer layer made of **calcium**. Inside each bone is a soft, **spongy** layer that looks like a honeycomb. The hollow spaces in the honeycomb are filled with **marrow**. Every minute, millions of **blood** cells die. But you don't need to worry. The bone marrow works like a little factory, making new blood cells for you.

Directions:

Use the highlighted words above to finish the sentences below.

1. Your skeleton _ _ _ _ _ _ _ _ your soft organs.
                      5

2. Bone _ _ _ _ _ _ makes new blood cells.
           2

3. Inside the bone is a soft, _ _ _ _ _ _ layer.
                                    3

4. Millions of _ _ _ _ _ cells die every minute.
                 4

5. The hard, outer layer of bone is made from _ _ _ _ _ _ _ .
                                                          1

6. More than two hundred bones are in your _ _ _ _ _ _ _ _ .
                                                              6

7. Your skeleton is a place for _ _ _ _ _ _ _ to attach.
                                    7

8. Your skeleton gives your body its _ _ _ _ _ .
                                        8

Challenge

What do you call a skeleton that won't get out of bed? Use the numbered letters above to find out. _ _ z _ _ _ _ _ _
                                                                           1 2 3   4 5 6 7 8

Human Body

Name _____

Your Pizza's Path

The organs of the digestive system work together to gain fuel from the foods we eat. Food is broken down into simple substances the body can use. These substances are absorbed into the bloodstream and any leftover waste matter is eliminated.

When you eat pizza (or any food), each bite you take goes through a path in the human body called the **alimentary canal**, or the digestive tract. This canal consists of the mouth, esophagus, stomach and small and large intestines. It is in this path that foods are broken down, vitamins are saved and poisons are discarded.

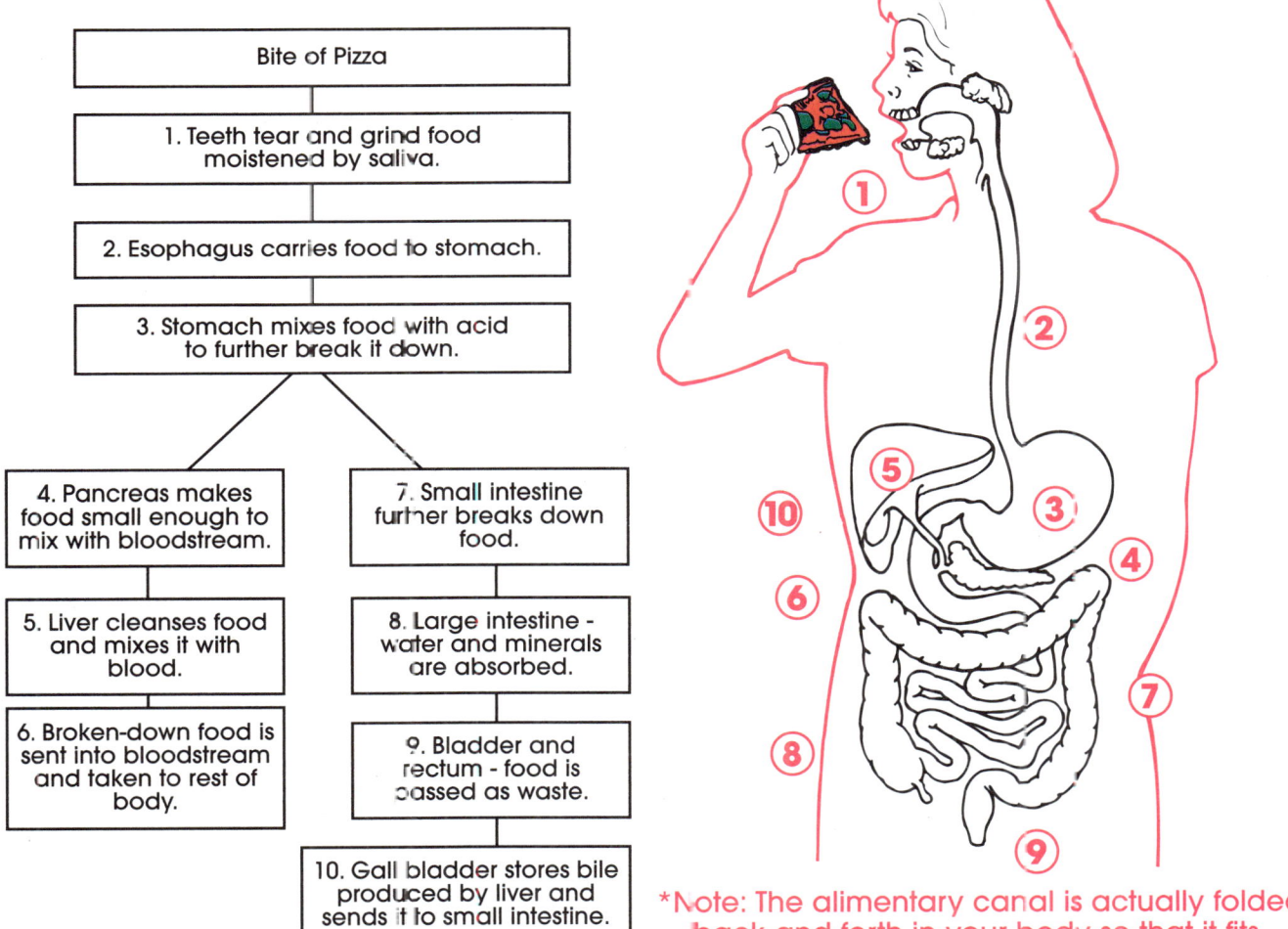

*Note: The alimentary canal is actually folded back and forth in your body so that it fits.

1. Name 3 parts of the pizza that are healthy. _____
2. Use a black crayon to trace the path of the healthy parts of the pizza.
3. Name 3 parts of the pizza that are unhealthy. _____
4. Use a blue crayon to trace the path of the unhealthy parts of the pizza.

Human Body

Name _____

Breathing Tree

Did you know that you have a tree inside your chest? This tree has a special job. It takes air from your windpipe and spreads it all through your lungs. This tree is called your **bronchial tree**.

Air enters through your **nose**. It passes over the hairs inside your nose. This warms and cleanses the air. Then, it travels down your **windpipe** until it comes to your bronchial tree. The bronchial tree divides into two tubes. One tube sends air into your right **lung**. The other tube sends air into your left lung.

Inside the lungs, the air fills almost 300 million tiny, spongy **air sacs**. These air sacs give fresh **oxygen** to the blood. At the same time, they take away **carbon dioxide** from the blood. Carbon dioxide is the air that has already been used. When you exhale, the carbon dioxide flows up the bronchial tree and out of your mouth and nose. The nose, windpipe, bronchial tree, lungs and air sacs work as a team. The team is called the **respiratory system**.

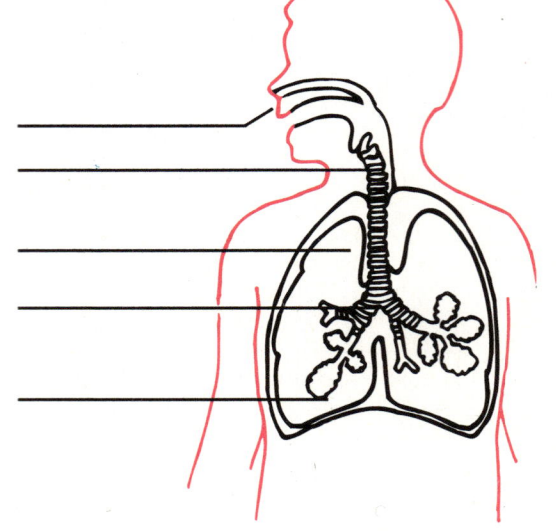

Label the parts of the respiratory system.

Who am I?

Inhale these scrambled words. Exhale the answers to the riddles.

1. I warm and clean the air you breathe. SNOE _____

2. There are 300 million of me in your lungs. RAI SCAS _____

3. You breathe me out. RONBAC DOXEIDI _____

4. I am your special tree. CHONRBALI REET _____

5. I am a long tube connecting your mouth to your lungs. DINWIPPE _____

6. I go through the air sacs and into the blood. YXONEG _____

Investigate
Smoking is harmful to your lungs. How can smoking affect breathing?

Human Body

Name _____

Your Body's Pipeline

Blood travels through three kinds of tubes. **Arteries** carry oxygen-rich blood from your heart to other parts of your body. Blood vessels, called **veins**, carry carbon dioxide-rich blood back to your heart. **Capillaries** are tiny vessels that connect arteries and veins. Capillaries take carbon dioxide from the cells and give the cells oxygen. Capillaries are fifty times thinner than a hair. They are so small that the blood cells must line up one at a time to travel through them.

Your heart, blood, arteries, veins and capillaries work as a team. This team is called your **circulatory system**.

Directions:

Name three kinds of blood vessels.

1. _____

2. _____

3. _____

The picture shows your circulatory system.

1. Color the veins **blue**.
2. Color the arteries **red**.
3. Color the heart **brown**.

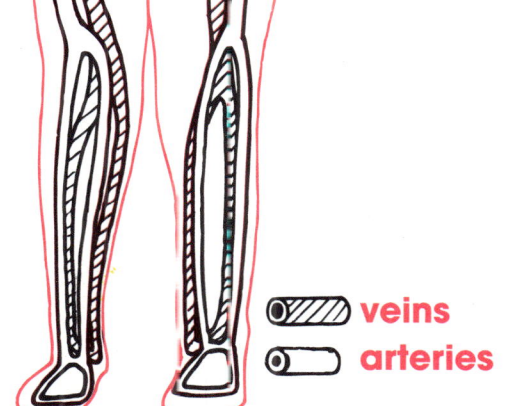

veins
arteries

Fantastic Fact
With every beat of your heart, blood starts a fantastic journey. Your blood travels through 60,000 miles of blood vessels to all the cells in your body.

Human Body

Lub-Dub, Lub-Dub

Place your hand on the left side of your chest. *Lub-dub, lub-dub*. Did you feel it? This is your heart pumping oxygen-rich blood to all parts of your body.

Your heart is really two pumps. It is divided down the middle. Each half of the heart is divided into two chambers. The **right half** pumps blood filled with a waste called carbon dioxide gas into the lungs. The **left half** of the heart takes oxygen-rich blood from the lungs. It sends the oxygen-rich blood to the cells in your body.

What about lub-dub? These are the sounds made by the little "trap doors" called **valves**. The valves open and close to let the blood flow in and out of the heart.

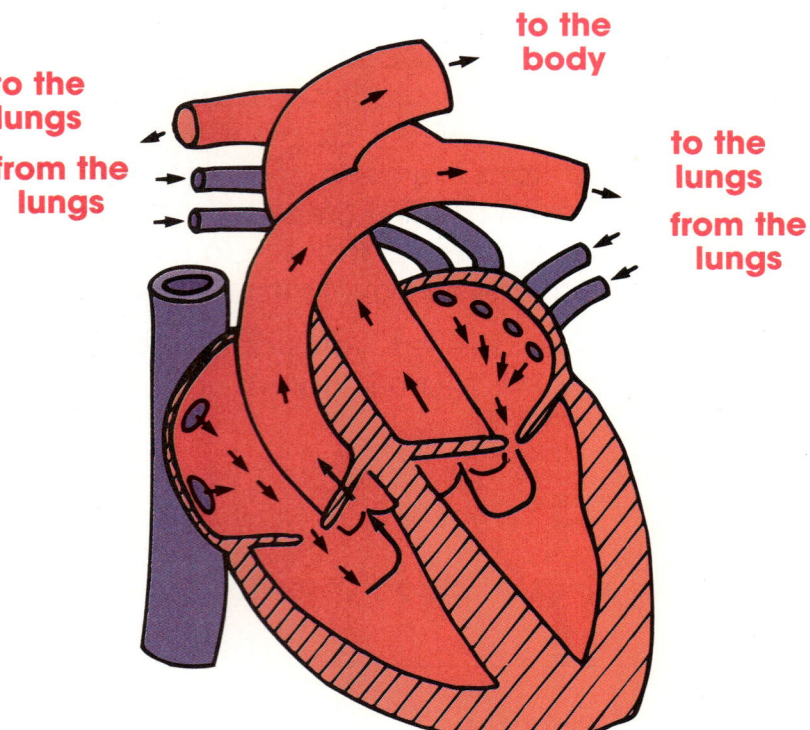

The arrows show the direction of blood flowing through the heart.

Directions:

Answer the questions below, using the information from above.

1. How many pumps does your heart have? _____

2. Where does the right half pump its blood? _____

3. Where does the left half pump its blood? _____

4. Which part of the heart makes the lub-dub sound? _____

Human Body

Name_____

Think Tank

Your brain has a very important job. It must keep your body working smoothly all day and night.

Your brain has three parts. The **cerebrum** is the largest part. It controls your body movement, such as running, walking, jumping, throwing a ball, holding a fork and other actions. It controls your five senses: hearing, smelling, tasting, seeing and touching. The cerebrum also controls your thinking and speaking.

The cerebrum is divided into two halves. The right half controls movements in the left side of your body. The left half controls movements in the right side of your body.

The part below the cerebrum is the **cerebellum**. The cerebellum makes sure that all of your muscles work together the way they should. It also helps you keep your balance.

The third and smallest part of the brain is the **brain stem**. The brain stem's job is extremely important. It controls breathing and the beating of your heart.

Directions: Label the three major parts of the brain.

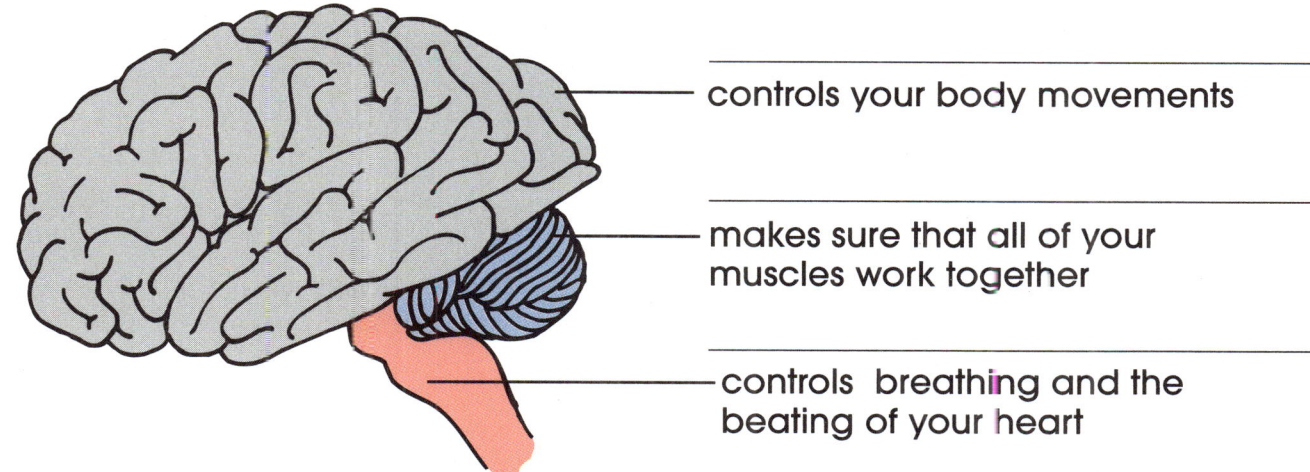

_____ controls your body movements

_____ makes sure that all of your muscles work together

_____ controls breathing and the beating of your heart

1. Which part of the skeleton protects the brain from injury?
2. Give the common name and the scientific name.
   common name:_____ scientific name:_____

Fantastic Fact
In order to function properly, the brain must have a constant supply of blood. The blood provides oxygen and other vitamins and nutrients needed by the brain to stay healthy.

Human Body   Name _____

Your Body's Messenger Service

Did you know that your nervous system has its own messenger service? Billions of tiny nerve cells throughout your body send messages to your brain.

First, the tiny nerve cells send their message to the spinal cord. (The **spinal cord** is a thick bundle of nerves running down the middle of your back.) Next, the spinal cord carries the message to your brain. Your brain reads the message and sends a new message back to your muscles. The new message tells your muscles how to move.

Think Fast!

How fast do you react to brain messages? Place your hand flat on a table. Have a friend hold an eraser about 1 ft. above your hand. Try to pull your hand away before your friend can drop the eraser on it.

Try five times and record each result.

Put a (✓) in either the "**hit**" or "**miss**" box.

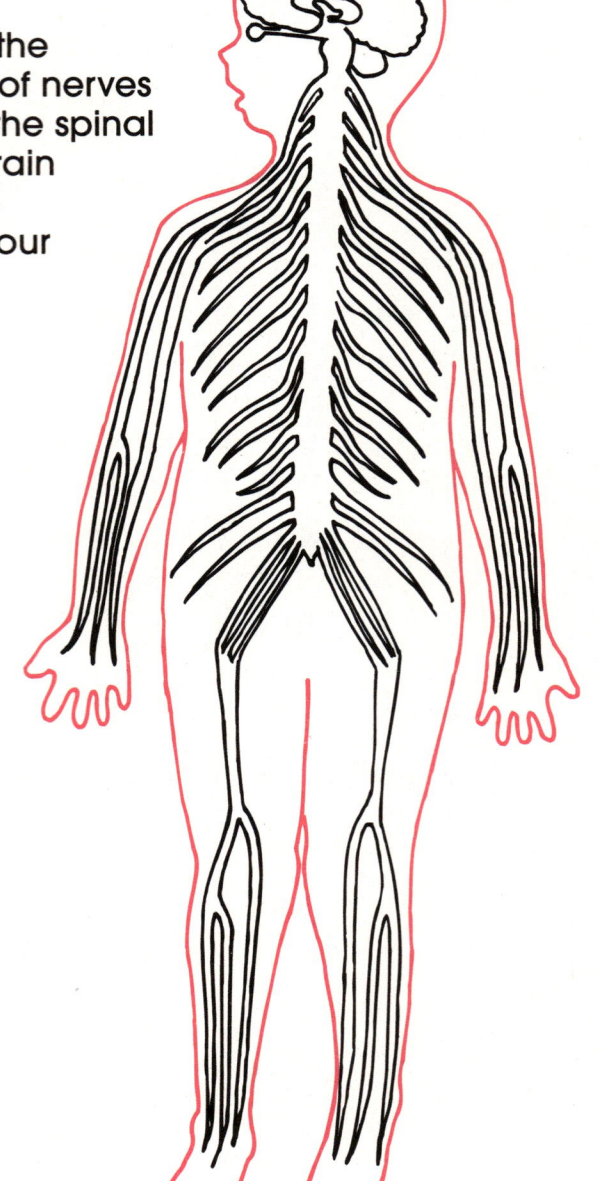

	#1	#2	#3	#4	#5
Hit					
Miss					

Color the parts of the nervous system.

brain - **gray**
spinal cord - **blue**
nerves - **red**

Investigate
What are some occupations that require a quick reaction time?

Nutrition

Name _____

You Are What You Eat!

You are not made out of pickles and carrots. The food you eat must be digested before your body can use it. Digested food is changed into nutrients which help your body grow and give you energy.

Unscramble the names of the six nutrient groups. Use the Word Bank.

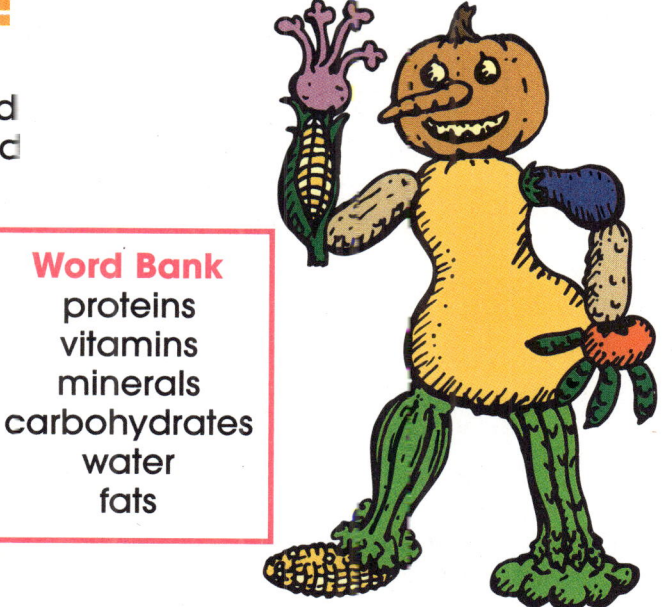

Word Bank
proteins
vitamins
minerals
carbohydrates
water
fats

netroips _____

ralmenis _____

afts _____

ratew _____

timnivas _____

droracbaytesh _____

Nutrient Job Board

Match each nutrient from above with the job that it does for your body.
(**Hint:** Look back at pages 120-122 for help.)

Needed: Nutrient to Deliver Food and Waste	Wanted: Muscle Builder and Body Repair Worker	Wanted: Nutrient to Store Energy
_____	_____	_____
Needed: Quick Energy Supplier	Needed: Growth and Good Health Helper	Needed: Nutrients for Many Jobs
_____	_____	_____

Investigate:
How much of your body is water?

Published by Frank Schaffer Publications. Copyright protected.

Science: Grade 3

Nutrition

Name _____

Tasty Plant Parts

All of the fruits and vegetables you eat come from plant parts. Some parts are much tastier than others. Carrot roots probably taste better than walnut tree roots.

Directions: Unscramble the names of the plant parts and label the pictures.

ealf_____   truif_____   frowel_____

smet_____   toors_____   eseds_____

Extension:
Garbage Gardening

1. Collect and wash the seeds from some fresh fruits and vegetables such as pumpkins, apples or beans.
2. Soak the seeds overnight.
3. Plant the seeds ½ inch deep in a container of potting soil.
4. Keep the soil moist and in a warm place.
5. Watch for the seedlings!

Plants   Name _____

Plant Parts

Green, flowering plants grow all around you. Beautiful red roses, tall cornstalks or prickly thistle weeds are all green, flowering plants. Green, flowering plants have six parts: **stem**, **root**, **leaf**, **flower**, **fruit** and **seeds**.

Directions: Complete the word puzzle. Then, use the words from the puzzle to label the plant.

Across:
1. I often have bright colors, but my real job is to make seeds.
3. I carry water from the roots to the leaves and food back to the roots.
4. I collect energy from the sun to make food for the plant.

Down:
1. I often taste delicious, but my job is to hold and protect the seeds.
2. I hold the plant tight like an anchor, but also collect water and minerals from the soil.
3. Someday a new plant will grow from me.

Fantastic Facts
The American Indians used every part of the sunflowers they grew. They ate the root and fed the stem and leaves to their animals. They ground the seeds for meal flour and used the yellow petals for dye. They even used the oil from the seeds for their hair.

Plants

Slurp, Slurp

Slurp, slurp! On a hot summer day, a cherry soda is cool and refreshing. Plants like to drink, too. The plant's root system slurps water and **minerals** from the ground. There are **two** kinds of root systems. Some plants have one main root that grows deep into the ground. This is called a **tap** root. Other plants have shallow roots with many **branches**. These roots are called **fibrous** roots. Attached to both root systems are tiny root **hairs** that do all the work of absorbing water.

Directions: Color the tap root **orange**. Color the fibrous roots **brown**. Write the name of the root system in the blank space. Label the root hairs.

Use the highlighted words to complete the word puzzle. Then, find the mystery word in the puzzle.

1. The _____ root grows deep into the ground.
2. Roots "slurp" water and _____ .
3. Fibrous roots have many _____ .
4. Tiny root _____ absorb water.
5. There are _____ types of root systems.
6. _____ roots grow shallow.

Use the mystery word in the puzzle to solve the riddle.

A ship's is made of iron,
To hold it fast at berth.
A plant's roots work like one,
To hold it firm in the earth.

What is it? _____

Fantastic Fact
The American Indians boiled the balsam root to make tea. They drank the tea when they had a sore throat, cough, pneumonia or hay fever.

Plants

Tree-mendous Plant

What is the largest plant growing near your home? It is probably a tree. It may be a maple, oak, pine or palm. All trees have many of the same parts as the plants that grow in your garden— only much larger.

The riddles below tell about the jobs of the tree parts. Use the tree parts listed in the Word Bank to solve each riddle. Then, label the parts of the tree.

Word Bank
seed
trunk
leaves
roots
bark

- Green and flat
  Or needle-like,
  We make food by day
  And rest at night.
  _____

- From roots to branches,
  Short or long,
  My tough wood
  Keeps me tall and strong.
  _____

- Scattered by wind
  When breezes blow,
  I'll make a new tree
  When I sprout and grow.
  _____

- Thin-like hair,
  Or thick and round,
  We hold the tree
  Firmly in the ground.
  _____

- Rough or smooth,
  A very tough cover,
  I keep out insects,
  Fire and weather.
  _____

Investigate
Very few trees have smooth bark. Find out why most bark is rough and has scales or cracks.

Plants

Leaves or Needles

Everyone has seen trees, but how do you tell one kind of tree from another? Trees have different leaves, seeds, bark and flowers. There are two main kinds of trees. The **conifers** are trees with needle-like leaves. Their seeds are found in cones. Conifers stay green all year long. The **broad-leaved** trees have leaves of different sizes and shapes. Broad-leaved trees often lose their leaves in the fall. In warm regions, some broad-leaved trees keep their leaves all year long.

Find the hidden names of conifer trees in the conifer tree. Find the hidden names of broad-leaved trees in the broad-leaved tree. Use the Word Bank to help you.

Word Bank

oak	ash
pine	elm
beech	spruce
redwood	cedar
fir	maple

1. _____
2. _____
3. _____
4. _____
5. _____

1. _____
2. _____
3. _____
4. _____
5. _____

Directions: Solve the word puzzle.

Across:

2. Conifers stay ____ all year long.
3. Broad-leaved trees lose their leaves in the ____.
4. Conifer seeds are in ____.

Down:

1. Conifer leaves are shaped like ____.

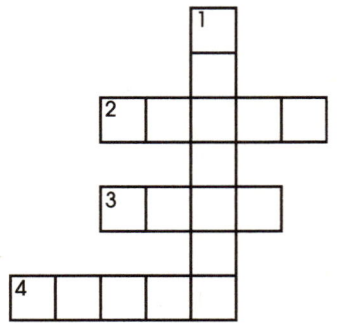

Plants Name _____

How Does Your Garden Grow?

Experience planting, caring for, harvesting and packaging vegetables by planting a small garden of radishes.

You will need:

paper cups
radish seeds
potting soil

Directions:

1. Fill the paper cups three-fourths full with soil.

2. Plant radish seeds according to the package directions. (Radishes are great for this activity as they are fast-growing vegetables, and you will be able to harvest them within 20-30 days.)

3. When they are ready to harvest, or pull, wash them and package them in sandwich bags. Enjoy!

Extension:
Throughout the care and growth of vegetable production, discuss the various ways in which vegetables are packaged. Have samples of fresh, frozen, canned and dried vegetables available to examine. Discuss where each should be stored.

Published by Frank Schaffer Publications. Copyright protected.   Science: Grade 3

Plants

Cruising Coconuts

Name _____

"Look at this coconut!" Amy called to Matt as they walked along the beach. Safe inside its thick husk, the coconut had floated across the water. Once it washed up on shore, the green leaves sprouted from this large seed.

Seeds travel in many ways. Below are five ways that seeds travel. Tell how each seed travels.

_____
_____
_____
_____
_____
_____
_____
_____
_____
_____
_____
_____
_____
_____

Fantastic Fact
Blast Off—The seed pod of the "touch-me-not" swells as it gets ripe. Finally, the seed pod bursts and launches seeds in all directions.

Solar System

Name _____

The Solar System

Our **solar system** is made up of the sun and all the objects that go around, or **orbit**, the sun.

The sun is the only star in our solar system. It gives heat and light to the nine planets in the solar system. The planets and their moons all orbit the sun.

The time it takes for each planet to orbit the sun is called a **year**. A year on Earth is 365 days. Planets closer to the sun have shorter years. Their orbit is shorter. Planets farther from the sun take longer to orbit, so their years are longer. A year on Pluto is 248 of our years!

Asteroids, comets and meteors are also part of our solar system.

Draw the nine planets around the sun.

Underline:

The solar system is: the sun without the nine planets.
                       the sun and all the objects that orbit it.

Check:

☐ is the center of our solar system.
☐ is the only star in our solar system.
☐ is a planet in our solar system.
☐ gives heat and light to our solar system.

Write:

A _____ is the time it takes for a planet to orbit the sun.
   month   year

Match:

Planets closer to the sun . . .   have a longer year.
Planets farther from the sun . . .   have a shorter year.

Solar System

Name _____

Spinning Top

Whir-r-r-ling! Matt's top is spinning very fast. Just like Matt's top, the Earth is also spinning.

The Earth spins about an imaginary line that is drawn from the North **Pole** to the South Pole through the center of the Earth. This line is called Earth's **axis**. Instead of using the word "spin," though, we say that the Earth **rotates** on its axis.

The Earth rotates **one** time every 24 hours. The part of the Earth facing the sun experiences day. The side that is away from the sun's light experiences **night**.

Draw a line from each picture of Matt to the correct day or night picture of the Earth.

Directions:
Use the highlighted words above to solve the puzzle.

1. The part of the Earth not facing the sun experiences _____.
2. Earth's axis goes from the North to the South _____.
3. The Earth spins, or _____.
4. Number of times the Earth rotates in 24 hours.
5. Imaginary line on which the Earth rotates.

Fantastic Fact
At the Equator, the Earth is spinning at a speed of almost 1,000 miles per hour. At a point halfway between the poles and the Equator, the speed is about 800 miles per hour. Spin a globe and you will see how this happens.

Solar System

Space Shadows

Have you ever held your hand up in front of a bright light to make shadow pictures on the wall? The sun and moon can cast shadows on the Earth just like the light and your hand cast shadow pictures on the wall.

Sometimes the moon passes between the Earth and the sun in just the right place to cast a shadow on the Earth. The sky darkens. The air becomes cooler. It seems like the middle of the night. This is called a **solar eclipse**.

Directions:

Write "solar eclipse" on the picture which best shows one.

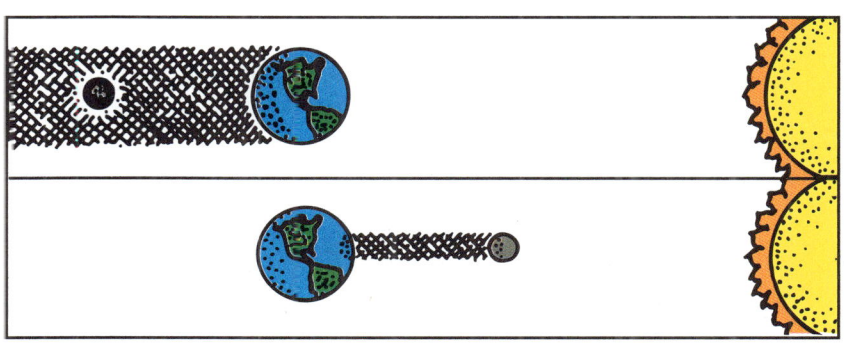

The moon casts an eerie shadow on the Earth during a solar eclipse. Ordinary objects can also cast eerie shadows when the light hits them at different angles. Circle the object that formed the shadow.

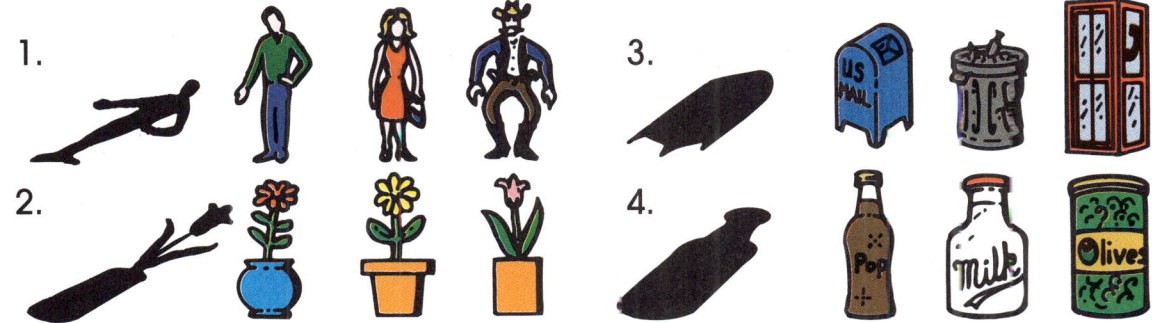

Draw a shadow for the objects below.

Published by Frank Schaffer Publications. Copyright protected.   Science: Grade 3

Solar System

Name _____

How Big?

Planets vary greatly in size. Look at the list of planets and their **diameters**.

Planet	Diameter
Mercury	3,000 miles
Venus	7,500 miles
Earth	7,900 miles
Mars	4,200 miles
Jupiter	88,700 miles
Saturn	74,600 miles
Uranus	31,600 miles
Neptune	30,200 miles
Pluto	1,900 miles

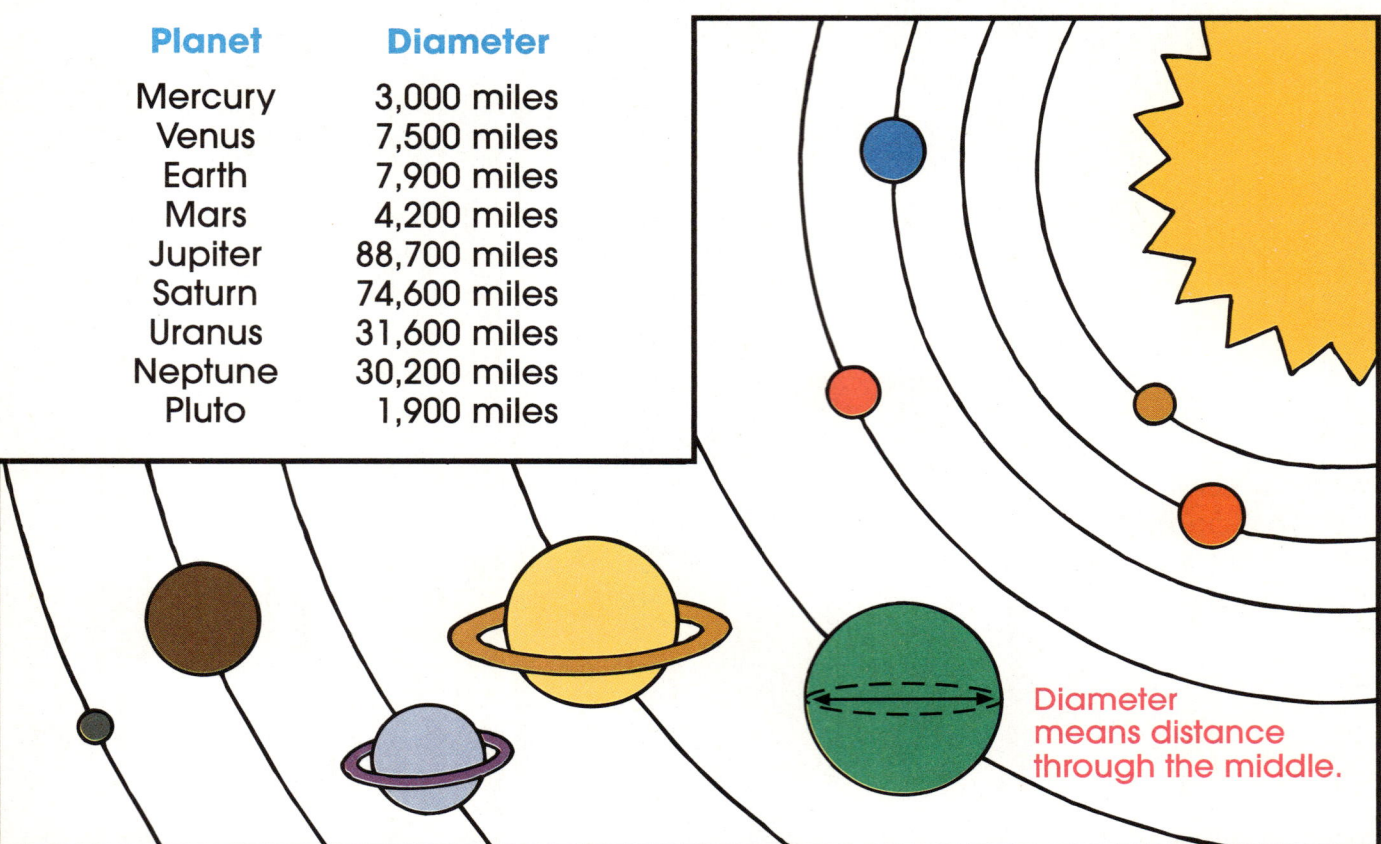

Diameter means distance through the middle.

Directions:

Write the names of the planets in order by size, starting with the planet that has the **largest** diameter.

1. _____
2. _____
3. _____
4. _____
5. _____
6. _____
7. _____
8. _____
9. _____

Solar System

Name _____

Mercury

Mercury is one of the smallest of the nine planets in our solar system. It is also the nearest planet to the sun.

Mercury spins very slowly. The side next to the sun gets very hot before it turns away from the sun. The other side freezes while away from the sun. As the planet slowly spins, the frozen side then becomes burning hot and the hot side becomes freezing cold.

Even though Mercury spins slowly, it moves around the sun very quickly. That is why it was named Mercury—after the Roman messenger for the gods.

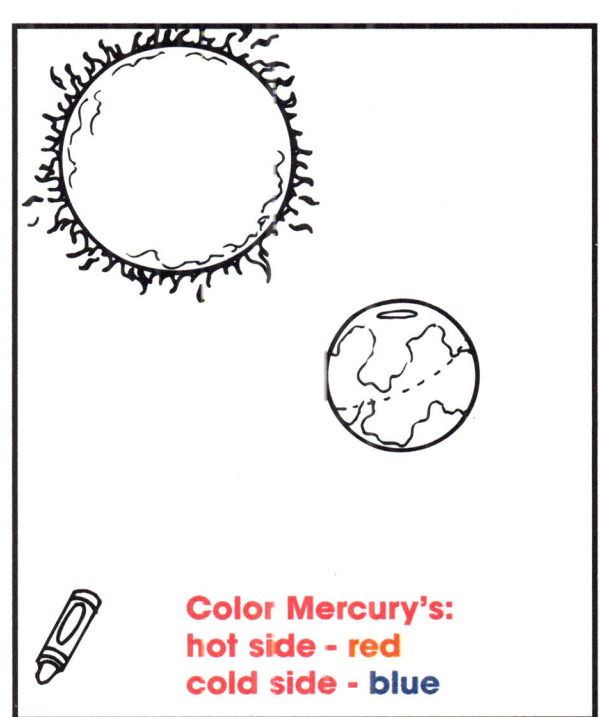

**Color Mercury's:
hot side - red
cold side - blue**

Underline:

Mercury   is the largest planet in our solar system.
           is one of the smallest planets in our solar system.

Write: darkest   nearest

Mercury is the_____ planet to the sun.

Match:

How does spinning slowly affect the temperature on Mercury?

    The side next to the sun   is freezing cold.
    The side away from the sun   is burning hot.

Circle:

Mercury moves   quickly   around the sun.   Mercury spins very   lightly.
                quietly   slowly.

Check:

Mercury was named for the   ☐ famous Roman speaker.
                            ☐ Roman messenger for the gods.

Solar System

Name _____

Venus

Venus is the planet nearest to Earth. Because it is the easiest planet to see in the sky, it has been called the **Morning Star** and **Evening Star**. The Romans named Venus after their goddess of love and beauty. Venus is sometimes called "Earth's twin."

Venus is covered with thick clouds. The sun's heat is trapped by the clouds. The temperature on Venus is nearly 900°F!

Space probes have been sent to study Venus. They have reported information to scientists. But they can only last a few hours on Venus because of the high temperature.

Venus turns in the opposite direction from Earth. So, on Venus, the sun rises in the west and sets in the east!

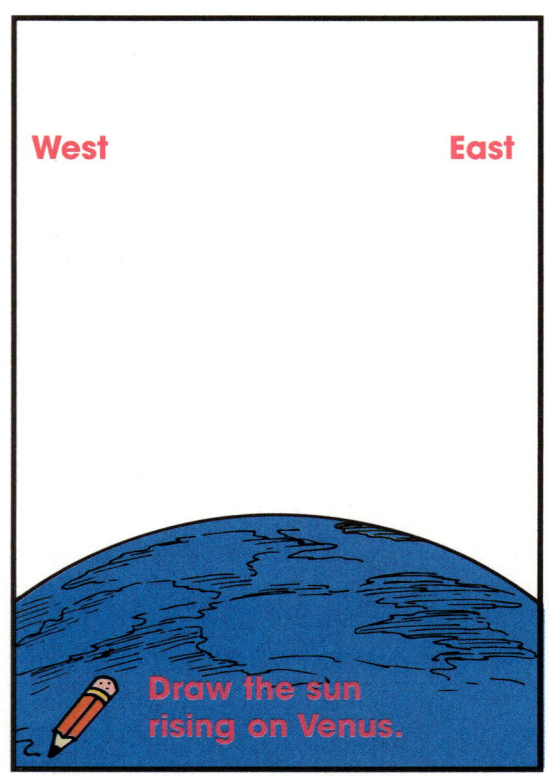

Unscramble and Circle:

_____ is the friendliest nearest planet to Earth.
  e s V u n
  2 5 1 4 3

Check:
It is called the
☐ Evening Sun
☐ Morning Star   because it is so easy to see.
☐ Evening Star

Circle:
The Romans named Venus for their:

goddess of love and beauty   god of light   goddess of truth

Circle Yes or No:

Half of Venus is frozen with ice and snow.	Yes	No
Space probes have reported information from Venus.	Yes	No
On Venus, the sun rises in the east and sets in the west.	Yes	No

Solar System

Mars

Mars is the fourth planet from the sun at 141,600,000 miles. The diameter of Mars is 4,200 miles. Mars is often called the Red Planet because rocks on its surface contain limonite, which is similar to rust. Mars has two moons.

Mars is dustier and drier than any desert on Earth. However, new evidence suggests that Mars may have once been a wetter and warmer planet. According to information gathered at the 1997 landing site of the Mars Pathfinder Mission, there may have been tremendous flooding on Mars about 2 to 3 billion years ago. Mars, then, may once have been more like Earth than was earlier thought.

Scientists are now pondering this question—if life was able to develop on Earth 2 to 3 billion years ago, why not on Mars too? What do you think about this? Explain your answer on the lines below.

_____
_____
_____
_____
_____
_____
_____
_____

Fantastic Fact
Morning temperatures on Mars are much different than on Earth. If you were standing on Mars, your nose would be at least 68°F colder than your feet!

Solar System

Name _____

Jupiter

Jupiter is the largest planet in our solar system. It has sixteen moons. Jupiter is the second-brightest planet—only Venus is brighter.

Jupiter is bigger and heavier than all of the other planets together. It is covered with thick clouds. Many loose rocks and dust particles form a single, thin, flat ring around Jupiter.

One of the most fascinating things about Jupiter is its Great Red Spot. The Great Red Spot of Jupiter is a huge storm in the atmosphere. It looks like a red ball. This giant storm is larger than Earth! Every six days it goes completely around Jupiter.

Draw and color the Great Red Spot circling Jupiter.

Unscramble and Write in Puzzle:

1. Jupiter is the _____ planet in our solar system.
   e t s l r g a
   5 7 6 1 3 4 2

2. Jupiter has _____ moons.
   t n x s e i e
   4 7 3 1 5 2 6

3. Jupiter is covered with thick _____.
   d s o c l u
   5 6 3 1 2 4

4. Loose rocks and dust form a _____ around Jupiter.
   g i r n
   4 2 1 3

5. The Great Red _____ of Jupiter is a huge storm.
   t s o p
   4 1 3 2

Circle and Write:

Jupiter is the second   largest / brightest   planet.

Jupiter is _____ and   lighter / heavier   than all of the planets together.
            bigger   redder

Published by Frank Schaffer Publications. Copyright protected.   Science: Grade 3

Solar System

Name _____

Saturn

Saturn is probably most famous for its rings. These rings are made of billions of tiny pieces of ice and dust. Although these rings are very wide, they are very thin. If you look at the rings from the side, they are almost too thin to be seen.

Saturn is the second-largest planet in our solar system. It is so big that 758 Earths could fit inside it!

Saturn is covered by clouds. Strong, fast winds move the clouds quickly across the planet.

Saturn has 18 moons! Its largest moon is called Titan.

Draw 18 moons around Saturn!

Circle:
Saturn is most famous for its

                                        spots.   rings.

Write:
Saturn's rings are made of _____ and _____.
                                      mud   ice   dust   moons

Check:
Saturn's rings are   ☐ red, yellow and purple.
                             ☐ wide, but thin.

Underline:

is the second-largest planet in our solar system.
is big enough to hold 758 Earths inside it.
is farther from the sun than any other planet.
is covered by fast, strong winds.
has 18 moons.

Unscramble:
Saturn's largest moon is called _____.
                                   i T a n t
                                   2 1 4 5 3

Solar System

Name _____

The Large Planets

Jupiter is about 88,836 miles at its equator. Named after the king of the Roman gods, it is the fifth-closest planet to the sun at about 483,600,000 miles away. Jupiter travels around the sun in an oval-shaped (elliptical) orbit. Jupiter also spins faster than any other planet and makes a complete rotation in about 9 hours and 55 minutes.

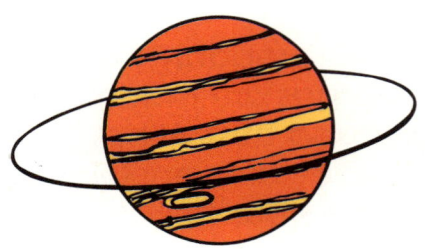

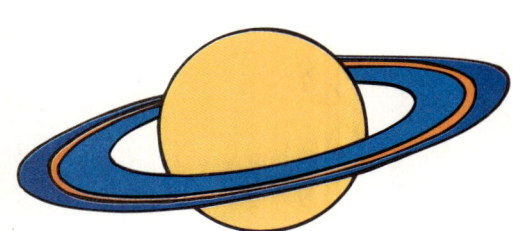

The surface of Jupiter cannot be seen from Earth because of the layers of dense clouds surrounding it. Jupiter has no solid surface but is made of liquid and gases that are held together by gravity.

One characteristic unique to Jupiter is the Great Red Spot that is about 25,000 miles long and about 20,000 miles wide. Astronomers believe the spot to be a swirling, hurricane-like mass of gas.

Saturn, the second-largest planet, is well known for the seven thin, flat rings encircling it. Its diameter is about 74,898 miles at the equator. It was named for the Roman god of agriculture. Saturn is the sixth planet closest to the sun and is about 888,200,000 miles away from it. Like Jupiter, Saturn also travels around the sun in an elliptical orbit, and it takes the planet about 10 hours and 39 minutes to make one rotation.

Scientists believe Saturn is a giant ball of gas that also has no solid surface. Like Jupiter, they believe it too may have an inner core of rocky material. Whereas Saturn claims 18 satellites, Jupiter has only 16 known satellites.

Directions: Fill in the chart below to compare Jupiter and Saturn. Make two of your own categories.

Categories	Jupiter	Saturn
1. diameter		
2. origin of name		
3. distance from sun		
4. rotation		
5. surface		
6. unique characteristics		
7.		
8.		

Solar System

Name _____

Uranus

Did you know that Uranus was first thought to be a comet? Many scientists studied the mystery comet. It was soon decided that Uranus was a planet. It was the first planet to be discovered through a telescope.

Scientists believe that Uranus is made of rock and metal with gas and ice surrounding it.

Even through a telescope, Uranus is not easy to see. That is because it is almost two billion miles from the sun that lights it. It takes Uranus 84 Earth years to orbit the sun! Scientists know that Uranus has fifteen moons and is circled by ten thin rings. But there are still many mysteries about this faraway planet.

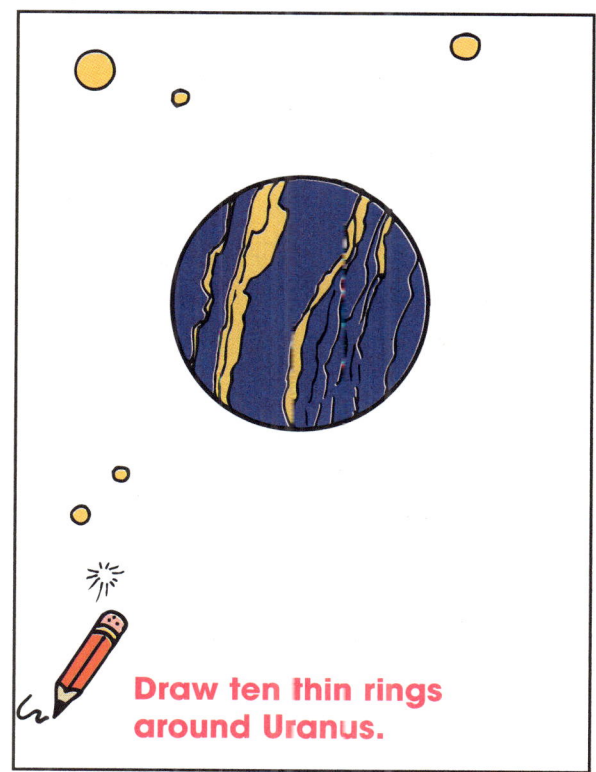

Draw ten thin rings around Uranus.

Circle:
Uranus was first thought to be a   moon.
   comet.

Write:
Uranus was the first planet to be discovered through a _____.
   telescope   TV

Check:
Scientists believe that Uranus is made of:

☐ rock   ☐ oil   ☐ metal   ☐ oceans   ☐ gas   ☐ ice

Match:

two billion miles ... the number of Uranus's moons
84 Earth years ... the distance of Uranus from the sun
fifteen ... the number of Uranus's rings
ten ... the time it takes Uranus to orbit the sun

Solar System

Name _____

Neptune

Neptune is the eighth planet from the sun. It is difficult to see Neptune—even through a telescope. It is almost three billion miles from Earth.

Scientists believe that Neptune is much like Uranus—made of rock, iron, ice and gases.

Neptune has eight moons. Scientists believe that it may also have several rings.

Neptune is so far away from the sun that it takes 164 Earth years for it to orbit the sun just once!

Scientists still know very little about this cold and distant planet.

Draw 8 moons around Neptune.

Write, Circle or Unscramble:

eptune is the   sixth / eighth   planet from the sun.

arth is almost three _____ miles from Neptune.
                                 million   billion

eople know   very little / very much   about Neptune.

elescopes are used to see Neptune.   **Yes   No**

ranus and Neptune are made of: rock   soap   gases   ice

eptune is a _____ and _____ planet.
            warm   cold   distant   near

very orbit around the _____ takes Neptune 164 Earth years.

Solar System　　　　　　　　　Name _____

The Twin Planets

1. Uranus and Neptune are similar in size, rotation time and temperature. Sometimes they are called twin planets. Uranus is about 1,786,400,000 miles from the sun. Neptune is about 2,798,800,000 miles from the sun. What is the difference between these two distances? _____

2. Neptune can complete a rotation in 18 to 20 hours. Uranus can make one in 16 to 18 hours. What is the average time it takes Neptune to complete a rotation? _____ Uranus? _____

3. Can you believe that it is about -353°F on Neptune, and about -357°F on Uranus? Brrr! That's cold! What is the temperature outside today in your town? _____
How much warmer is it in your town than on Neptune? _____ Uranus? _____

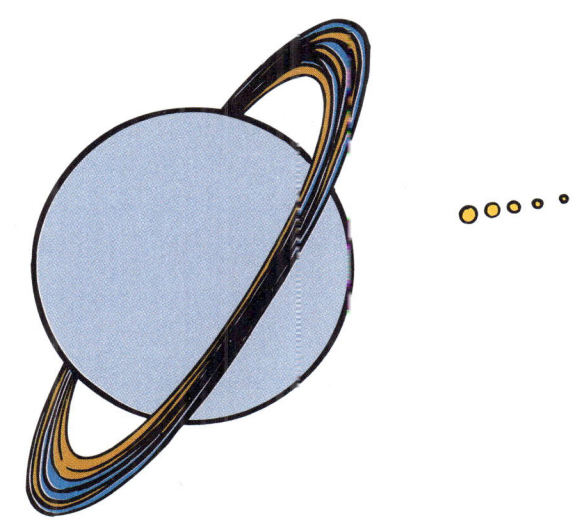

4. Uranus has at least five small satellites moving around it. Their names are Miranda, Ariel, Umbriel, Tatania and Oberon. They are 292, 721, 727, 982 and 945 miles in diameter, respectively. What is the average diameter of Uranus' satellites? _____

5. Neptune was first seen in 1846 by Johanna G. Galle. Uranus was first discovered by Sir William Herschel in 1781. How many years ago was Neptune discovered? _____ Uranus? _____
About how many years later was Uranus discovered than Neptune? _____

6. Both Uranus and Neptune have names taken from Greek and Roman mythology. Use an encyclopedia to find their names and their origins.

_____

_____

_____

Solar System

Pluto

Pluto is the ninth planet from the sun. It is farther from the sun than any other planet.

If you stood on Pluto, the sun would look just like a bright star in the sky. Pluto is so far away that it gets little of the sun's heat. That is why it is freezing cold on Pluto.

Some scientists think that Pluto was once one of Neptune's moons that escaped from orbit and drifted into space. Other scientists believe it has always been a planet in our solar system.

Pluto is so far away from the sun that it takes 247 Earth years just to orbit the sun once!

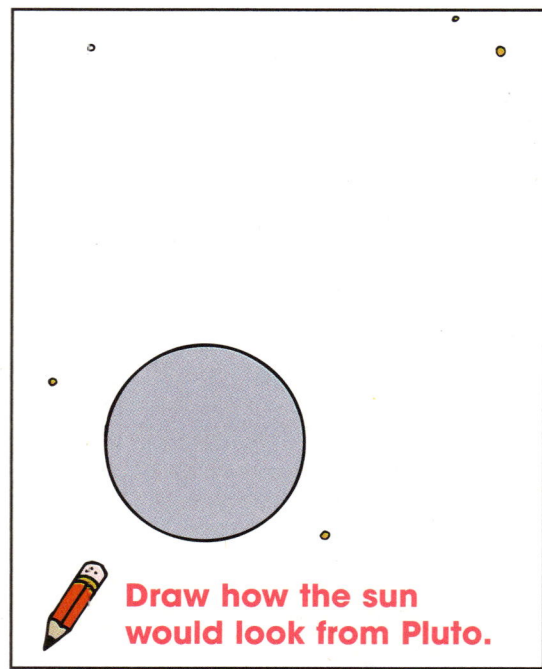

Draw how the sun would look from Pluto.

Unscramble and Circle:

_____ is the seventh / ninth planet from the sun.
l t P o u
2 4 1 5 3

Pluto is closer / farther from the _____ than any other planet.
n u s
3 2 1

Check:

Pluto Facts

☐ On Pluto, the sun looks like a bright star.
☐ Pluto gets very little of the sun's heat.
☐ Pluto has very hot weather.
☐ Pluto takes 247 Earth years to orbit the sun.

Circle:
Some scientists believe that Pluto was once Neptune's sun. / moon.

Solar System

Name _____

Read My Mind

Pretend you have been contacted by NASA to serve as an astronaut on a secret mission. Because of its secrecy, NASA cannot give you your destination. Instead, you must figure it out using the clues below. After each clue, check the possible answers. The planet with the most clues checked will be your destination.

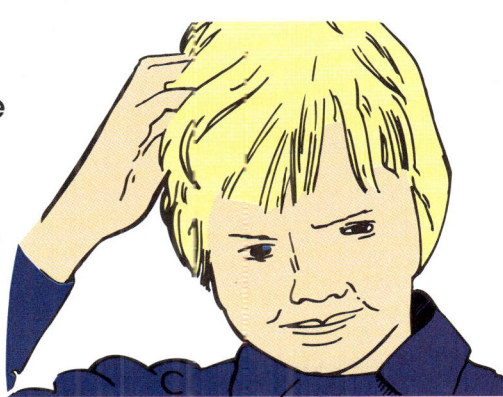

Destination Clues	Record Answers Here								
	Mercury	Venus	Earth	Mars	Jupiter	Saturn	Uranus	Neptune	Pluto
It is part of our solar system.									
It is a bright object in the sky.									
It is less than 2,000,000,000 miles from the sun.									
It orbits the sun.									
It has less than 15 known satellites.									
There is weather there.									
It rotates in the opposite direction of Earth.									
It is the hottest planet.									
Its years are longer than its days.									
It is called "Earth's twin."									
It is closest to Earth.									

Secret Mission Destination is _____
I know this because _____

Solar System

Name _____

The Milky Way Galaxy

The Milky Way galaxy is made up of the Earth, its solar system and all the stars you can see at night. There are over 100 billion stars in the Milky Way!

The Milky Way is shaped much like a C.D. It has a center which the outer part goes around.

The Milky Way is always spinning slowly through space. It is so large that it would take 200 million years for the galaxy to make one complete turn.

Many stars in the Milky Way are in clusters. Some star clusters contain up to one million stars!

Our solar system

Put a red circle around our solar system.

Check:
The Milky Way galaxy is made up of
☐ Earth.
☐ no sun.
☐ our solar system.
☐ 100 billion stars.

Circle Yes or No:

The Milky Way is shaped like a pencil.	Yes	No
The Milky Way is always slowly moving in space.	Yes	No
Many stars in the Milky Way are in clusters.	Yes	No
Some star clusters have one million stars.	Yes	No

Circle:

It would take   200
               90   million years for the galaxy to spin once.
               600

Underline.

Which object is the Milky Way shaped much like?

   C.D.      ruler

Solar System

Name _____

Weight and Gravity
Making a Scale

Directions:

1. Use a hole punch or scissors to punch two holes exactly opposite each other at the top of a clear plastic cup.
2. Cut a piece of fishing line 6" long. Tie one end to one hole and the other end to the opposite hole.
3. Tape a ruler to the top of a table so one end hangs over the edge. Then, tape a piece of tagboard to the side of the table.
4. Wrap a rubber band around the fishing line and loop it inside itself. Now hang the rubber band from the ruler. The cup should hang in front of the tagboard.

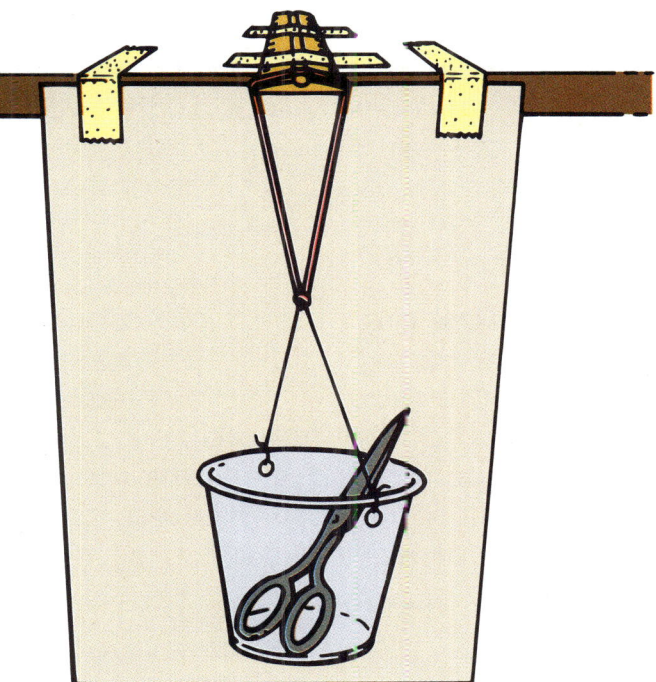

Comparing Weights

To weigh an object, place it in the cup. The heavier the object, the lower the cup will sag. To record its weight, put a mark on the tagboard even with the bottom of the cup and write the name of the object next to the mark.

Make a prediction. Put all the objects on the table. Line them up in order from the lightest to the heaviest. Now weigh the objects. Number them from lightest to heaviest, with 1 the lightest and 8 the heaviest.

____scissors   ____small jar of water   ____pencil   ____coin
____stone   ____crayon box   ____eraser   ____magnifying glass

How accurate was your prediction?

Extension:
Why is gravity important to humans? _____
_____
_____

What would happen if there were no gravity? _____
_____
_____

Solar System

Name _____

"Live Via Satellite"

"This program is brought to you live via satellite from halfway around the world." Satellites are very helpful in sending TV messages from the other side of the world. But this is only one of the special jobs that satellites can do.

Most satellites are placed into orbit around the Earth by riding on top of giant rockets. More recently some satellites have been carried into orbit by a space shuttle. While orbiting the Earth, the giant doors of the shuttle are opened, and the satellite is pushed into orbit.

This satellite relays TV signals from halfway around the world.

Satellites send information about many things. Use the code to find the different kinds of messages and information satellites send.

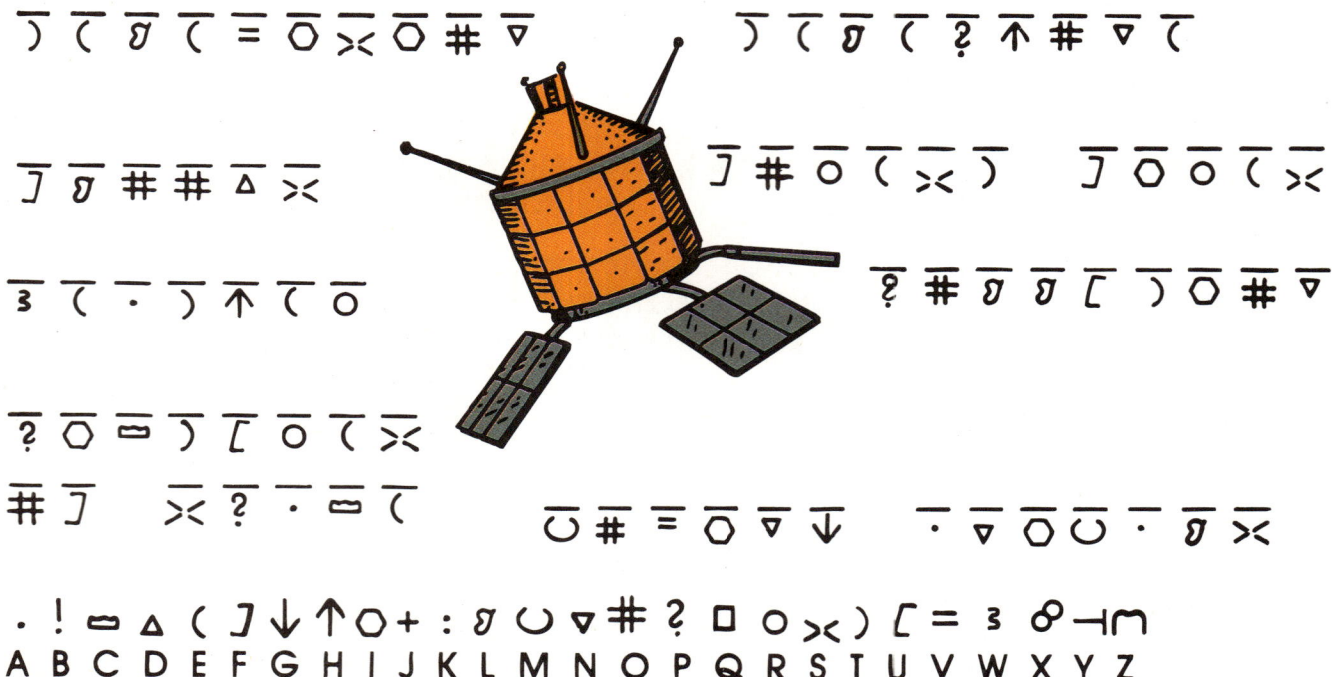

```
 .  !  ⊏  △  (  ]  ↓  ↑  ○  +  :  σ  ∪  ▽  #  ?  □  o  ⋈  )  [  =  3  8  ⊣  m
 A  B  C  D  E  F  G  H  I  J  K  L  M  N  O  P  Q  R  S  T  U  V  W  X  Y  Z
```

Investigate
Satellites in space need power to send messages. Find out where satellites get their power.

Weather

Name _____

Rain in the Rainforest

At least 80 inches of rain falls, and thundershowers may occur for 200 or more days each year in a rainforest. **Rainforests** need a lot of rain so that the plants native to them do not dry out. Fill in the precipitation graph below with the average rainfall of a typical tropical rainforest. The amounts are listed beneath the graph.

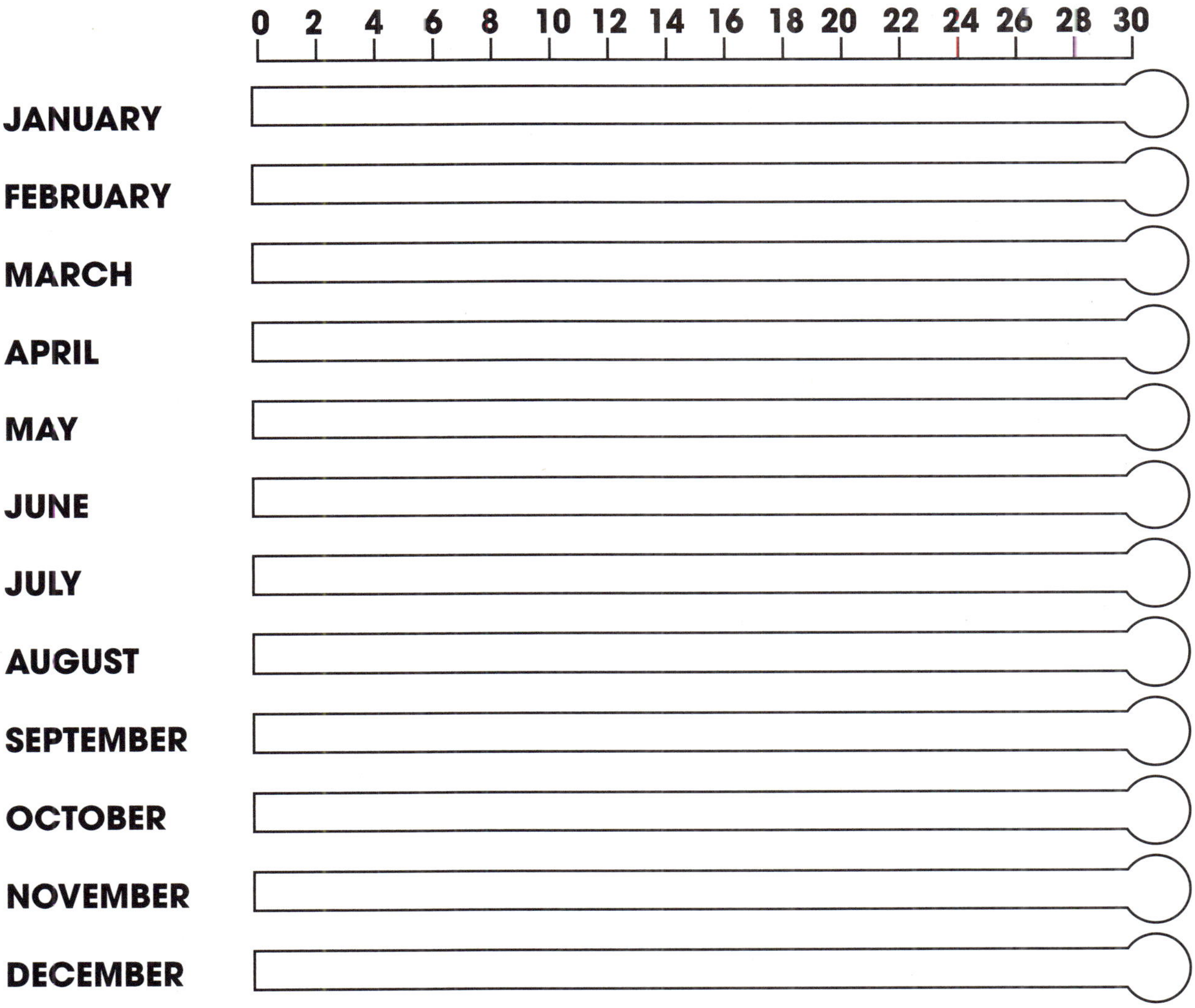

```
              0  2  4  6  8  10 12 14 16 18 20 22 24 26 28 30
```

JANUARY

FEBRUARY

MARCH

APRIL

MAY

JUNE

JULY

AUGUST

SEPTEMBER

OCTOBER

NOVEMBER

DECEMBER

J	F	M	A	M	J	J	A	S	O	N	D
24"	20"	13"	11"	10"	7"	8"	9"	9"	11"	14"	18"

What was the total rainfall for the year in this rainforest? _____

What is the total rainfall for a year in your area? _____

Weather

Name _____

Lightning

Lightning is a flash of light caused by electricity in the sky. Clouds are made of many water droplets. All of these droplets together contain a large electrical charge. Sometimes these clouds set off a large spark of electricity called **lightning**. Lightning travels very fast. As it cuts through the air, it can cause thunder.

Lightning takes various forms. Some lightning looks like a zigzag in the sky. Sheet lightning spreads and lights the sky. Ball lightning looks like a ball of fire.

Underline:

Lightning is a flash of light

1. caused by sunshine.
2. caused by electricity in the sky.

Circle Yes or No:

Sometimes clouds set off a huge spark of electricity.	Yes	No
Lightning is caused by dry weather.	Yes	No
Lightning travels very fast.	Yes	No
Lightning can cause thunder.	Yes	No

Unscramble and write in the puzzle above:

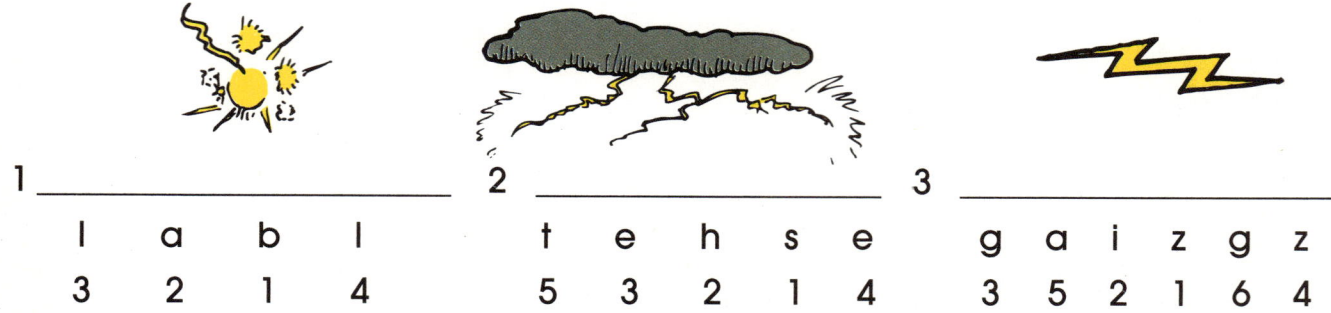

1 _____   2 _____   3 _____
   l a b l l   t e h s e   g a i z g z
   3 2 1 4   5 3 2 1 4   3 5 2 1 6 4

Draw a picture of a sky with the three kinds of lightning.

Weather

Name_____

A Funnel Cloud—Danger!

Did you know that a tornado is the most violent windstorm on Earth? A **tornado** is a whirling, twisting storm that is shaped like a funnel.

A tornado usually occurs in the spring on a hot day. It begins with thunderclouds and thunder. A cloud becomes very dark. The bottom of the cloud begins to twist and form a funnel. Rain and lightning begin. The funnel cloud drops from the dark storm clouds. It moves down toward the ground.

A tornado is very dangerous. It can destroy almost everything in its path.

Circle:

A  is the most violent windstorm on Earth.
(thunder / tornado)

Check:

Which words describe a tornado?

❏ whirling   ❏ twisting   ❏ icy   ❏ funnel-shaped   ❏ dangerous

Underline:

A funnel shape is: ○   □   ⬭   ▽   ⌇

Write and Circle:

A tornado usually occurs in the_____ on a cool / hot day.
                                    autumn   spring

Write 1 - 2 - 3 below and in the picture above.

◯ The funnel cloud drops down to the ground.

◯ A tornado begins with dark thunder clouds.

◯ The dark clouds begin to twist and form a funnel.

Weather

Name _____

Can You Pour Air?

Directions:

Lower a water glass (mouth downward) into a basin filled with water. Next, lower another glass of exactly the same size into the container of water. Tilt the second glass until it fills up with water. Still holding both glasses under water, turn the glass filled with water up so that the mouths of both glasses are together. Now, turn the first glass upward and watch the air pour from the first glass into the second. Holding both glasses under water, continue to pour the air from one glass into the other. Was either glass empty at any time?

Published by Frank Schaffer Publications. Copyright protected.

Science: Grade 3

Weather

Name _____

Cool Color

Does color have anything to do with temperature?

You will need:

2 identical glasses
one 9" x 12" sheet of black paper
one 9" x 12" sheet of white paper
masking tape
an index card
a pencil
a pen
an outside thermometer
water
scissors

Copy the Cool Color chart information onto the index card.

Cool Color

Name _____

Directions:

Wrap one glass with black paper and one with white paper. Tape the paper closed. Cut off the excess paper. Fill each glass with the same amount of water. Set both glasses in a sunny spot. Leave them there for at least an hour. Then, put the thermometer into each glass and record the temperature of each on the Cool Color chart. Also write on the chart what you concluded from this experiment. Do this experiment at least two more times to verify your conclusion. Try other colors to see if there is any difference.

Note: The water in the jar wrapped with black paper should be warmer because the black paper absorbs more heat than the white.

Magnets Name _____

The Invisible Force

Hold a magnet close to a piece of metal. Do you feel a pulling force? Magnets are attracted to certain metals. The invisible force is called **magnetism.**

What kinds of objects will a magnet pull? The best and the most fun way to find out is to experiment. Gather some of the objects listed below. Hold a small magnet next to these objects. Which objects will the magnet pull? Add some of your own objects to the list.

Object	Magnet Attracts	Magnet Does Not Attract
scissors		
wood ruler		
eraser		
paper clip		
thumbtack		
paper		
aluminum foil		

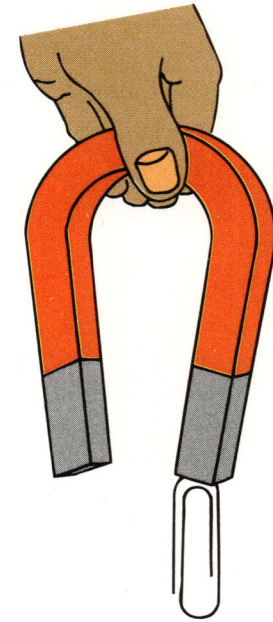

Magnets do not attract all metals. Find the six metals in the word search. The metals that are written "up and down" are attracted to magnets. The metals written "across" are not attracted. List each metal in the correct group.

```
B N B R A S S X
Z I K L N T I A
A C O P P E R D
N K T R O E O S
T E K G N L N P
A L U M I N U M
```

Attracted By Magnets

_____
_____
_____

Not Attracted By Magnets

_____
_____
_____

Fantastic Fact
Magnets were named after a shepherd called Magnes. According to legend, magnets were first discovered when Magnes stood on a rock. His sandals stuck to the rock when the nails in his sandals stuck to the "magic" rock. The magic rock was lodestone, a natural form of a magnet.

Earth

Out of This World

You will need:

an adult, 2 large bowls (one that can go in the freezer), a rolling pin, a wooden spoon, a large wooden cutting board, a saucepan, measuring spoons, a long sharp knife, paper plates, plastic forks, the ingredients listed below.

Cover the inside of the bowl that will go in the freezer with a nonstick spray.

INGREDIENTS:

Crust	4 tablespoons powdered sugar ½ cup butter 2 cups graham crackers
Mantle	½ cup crushed, unsalted peanuts chocolate ice cream
Outer Core	orange, red and yellow sorbet M&M's™
Inner Core	vanilla ice cream red and green food coloring

CRUST: Crush graham crackers on the cutting board. Mix powdered sugar with melted butter in a bowl. Line all sides of sprayed bowl with the mixture. Pat it inside the bowl to about ¼ - ½" thickness. Put it in the freezer until frozen.

Make layers in the order shown above, one layer at a time. Freeze each layer in the bowl before you go on to the next step. (Before mixing and adding each layer, let the ice cream soften, without completely melting.)

When the Earth's cross section is frozen, take it out of the freezer. Cut it in half and then in fourths. Remove one quarter at a time. Slice it like a cake so that each serving has a little of each of Earth's layers. Put it on plates and serve.

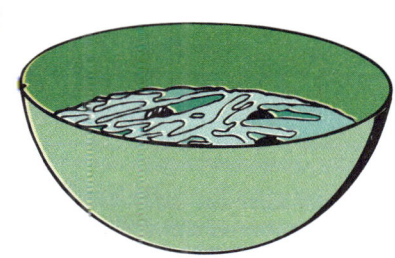

Earth   Name _____

Voom!

You will need:
vinegar, red food coloring, a large cardboard box, baking soda, a narrow plastic beaker, sand, a paper towel tube, scissors, clay, a flat box (3-4" high), an X-acto™ knife, masking tape

Cut and tape a flat box together so that it is about 10" square. Color the vinegar with red food coloring. Wear old clothes for the eruption.

Directions:

1. Fill half of a beaker with baking soda.

2. Cut two or three holes in the paper towel tube. Put it over the beaker.

3. Mold clay around the tube. Leave the top and the holes you poked open.

4. Make tunnels out of clay that lead down to the holes.

5. Put the beaker with the tube molded with clay in the large box. Pile damp sand around the clay volcano. Pat it to make it into a volcano shape. Leave the top and tunnels exposed.

6. When it is time to make it erupt, take it outside. Pour red vinegar into the beaker. Stand back. **VOOM!**

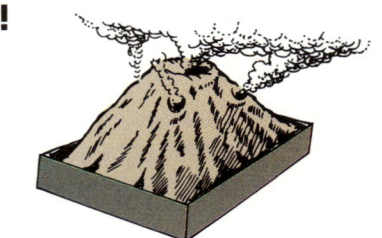

Magnets

Magnets

You will need:

a magnet
several objects made of various materials (i.e., paper clips, staples, rubber bands, paper fasteners, coins, aluminum foil, a gold ring, a silver ring, a piece of copper wire, several non-magnetic metals)
a marker
paper

Object	Magnetic	Non-Magnetic

Predict which objects would be attracted to a magnet. Draw a simple chart to classify your predictions (see above). Place the objects for which the predictions have been made in the correct column on the chart. After all the objects have been classified, test them with a magnet. Rearrange misclassified objects. Think about why these objects may have been misclassified. Scientific experiments are much more accurate than just guessing.

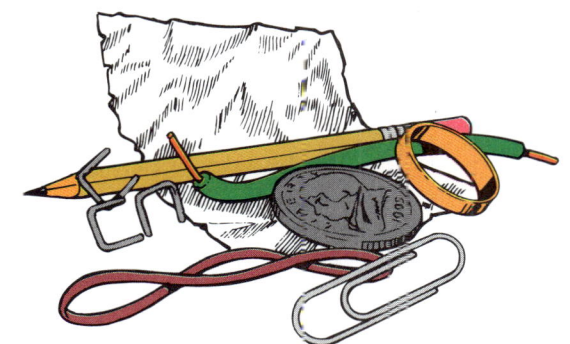

Magnetic Magician

The force of a magnet may pass through certain objects. Perform this activity to find out what materials work.

You will need: one strong magnet, paper clips, a sheet of paper, a piece of cardboard, a plate, a glass, a thin piece of wood, a piece of fabric, aluminum foil, a sheet of plastic, the lid of a large tin can, a plastic lid

Place some paper clips on the top of each of the materials listed above. Move a magnet under the materials. Watch to see if the magnet moves the clips through the paper, the wood, the glass, etc. If the clips can be moved, the force of the magnet is working through the material. Through experimentation, you will discover that magnetism will not pass through materials which are themselves magnetic. Why do you think this is so?

Simple Machines   Name _____

Push and Pull

Look at the children in the picture. How are they moving their friends? A push or a pull on something is called a **force**. Forces can cause an object to move, slow down, speed up, change direction or stop.

Directions:

You use pushing and pulling forces every day to move objects. List five ways that you use each of these forces.

Pushing Forces

1. _____
2. _____
3. _____
4. _____
5. _____

Pulling Forces

1. _____
2. _____
3. _____
4. _____
5. _____

It takes more force to move some objects than it does to move others. Circle the object in each picture which would take more force to move.

Published by Frank Schaffer Publications. Copyright protected.   Science: Grade 3

Simple Machines

Name _____

Machines of Old

Simple machines have been used for hundreds of years. The builders of the famous castles in Europe did not have modern machines. But they did have some simple machines to help them make their fabulous castles.

Directions:

Look carefully at the men building the castle. They are working hard, but their simple machines are missing. Draw in the missing machines. The Picture Bank at the bottom of the page will help you.

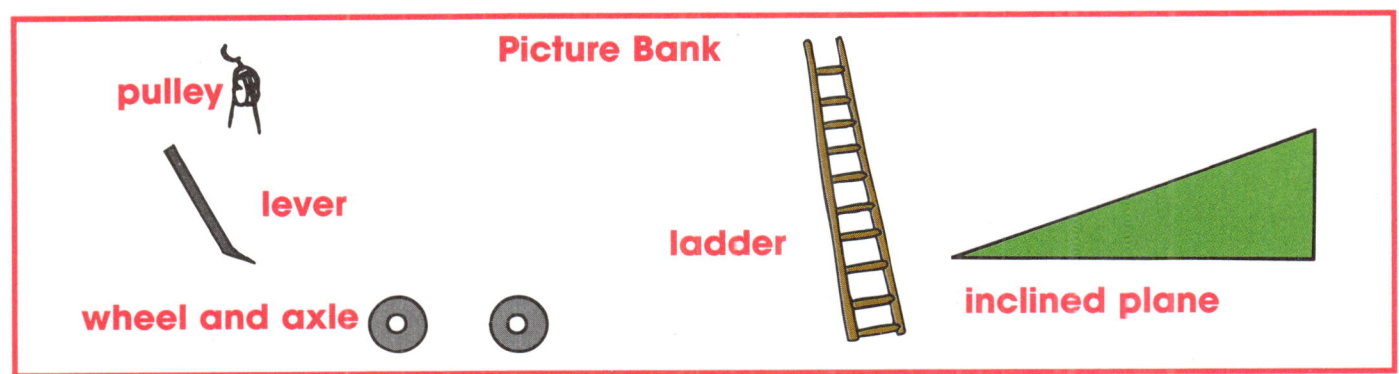

Simple Machines   Name _____

Around and Around

A doorknob is a simple machine you use every day. It is a **wheel and axle machine**. The wheel is connected to the axle. The axle is a center post. When the wheel moves, the axle does, too.

Opening a door by turning the axle with your fingers is very hard. But by turning the doorknob, which is the "wheel," you use much less force. The doorknob turns the axle for you. The doorknob makes it easy because it is much bigger than the axle. You turn the doorknob a greater distance, but with much less force.

Sometimes the "wheel" of a wheel-and-axle machine doesn't look like a wheel. But look at the path the doorknob makes when it is turned. The path makes a circle, just like a wheel.

Directions:

Color only the wheels of the wheel-and-axle machines below.

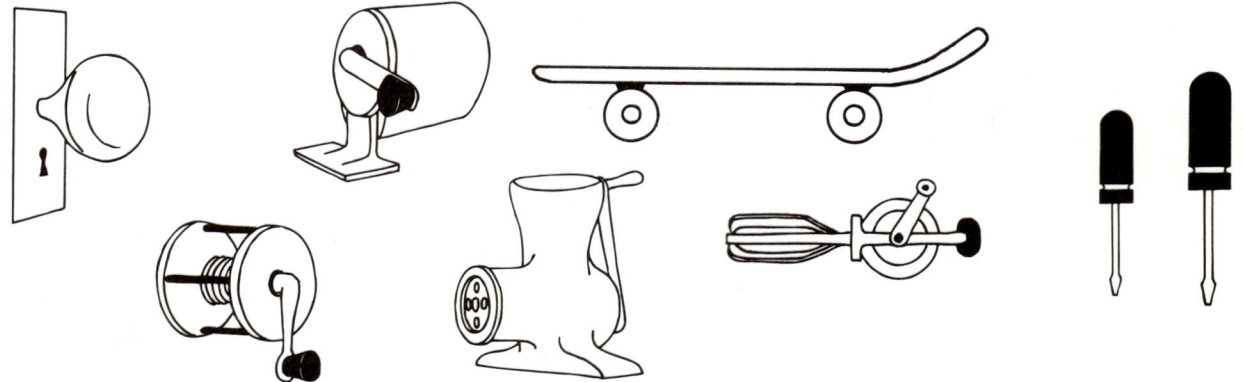

Look at the pictures above and answer these questions.

1. A screwdriver is a wheel and axle. What part of a screwdriver is the wheel?
   _____

2. What part of a screwdriver is the axle? _____

3. Which screwdriver has the largest wheel? _____

4. Which screwdriver would take the least amount of force to turn? _____

> **Challenge**
> Why is the crank on a meat grinder larger than the crank on a pencil sharpener? Why is the steering wheel on a truck larger than the steering wheel on a car?

Simple Machines

Name _____

Gearing Up

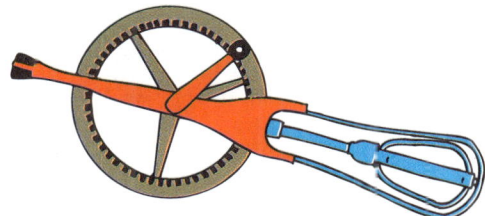

An eggbeater has a special kind of wheel. It is called a gear. A **gear** is a wheel with teeth. The teeth allow one gear to turn another gear.

Gears are often used to increase or decrease speed. If the large gear in the picture turns one time, how many times will the small gear turn?

Directions:

Gears are found in many machines. Circle all of the machines you can find in the puzzle. Then, list only the machines that use gears.

```
S T K N Z O R K G
H A M M E R U T K
O P S O R E R C N
V G Z V F A O T S
E B O I C L G X Z
L Z N E C B Z E K
D K X P W I Y G L
C K T R U C K G K
R R M O X Y T B G
A T N J S C U E H
K N R E R L V A Z
E G S C Q E W T R
P L K T G Z T E S
Z K P O H O X R T
Z U T R A M P N P
```

Machines with Gears

_____
_____
_____
_____
_____
_____
_____
_____

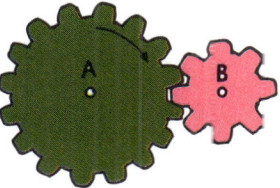

Look at the picture to the right.
1. Draw an arrow on the picture showing the direction gear **B** will turn.

2. If gear **A** is turned one time, how many times will gear **B** turn? _____

Challenge
Look at the gears to the right. What will happen if gear **A** is turned?

Simple Machines   Name _____

Ramps, Hills and Slopes

Word Bank	
machine	easier
force	inclined
shorter	longer

Directions:

Fill in the blanks with words from the Word Bank.

Simple machines help people do work. In the picture above, the ramp makes the man's work a lot _____. The ramp is a simple _____ called an inclined plane.

An _____ plane makes work easier. It lessens the amount of force needed to move a load. By using the ramp, the man moves the barrel with much less force than if he tried to lift the barrel himself. With the ramp, the man moves the barrel a _____ distance, but with much less force. By just lifting the barrel onto the truck, he would move it a _____ distance, but would need to use much more _____.

Ramps are used in many places to help people in wheelchairs get around more easily. List some places where ramps are used in your community.

1. _____
2. _____
3. _____

The angle of an inclined plane affects the amount of force needed to lift an object. The longer and less steep the inclined plane is, the less force it takes to lift an object.

Study the pictures below and then answer the questions.

1. On which ramp will the barrel have to travel the farthest to get on the truck?___

2. On which ramp will the least amount of force be needed to roll the barrel onto the truck?___

3. How does the angle of the ramp affect the force needed to move the barrel?
_____

Investigate
How did the early Egyptians use inclined planes to build the great pyramids?

Simple Machines   Name _____

Special Inclined Plane — Wedge

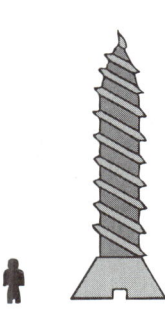

"Poof!" Leroy just shrank himself again in his "Super Electro Shrinking Machine." He is trying to decide which would be easier—climbing around and around the threads of a screw to get to the top or just climbing straight up the side of the screw. He found that the distance up the winding ramp is a lot farther, but the traveling is much easier than going straight up the side. The winding ramp of the screw is like a spiral stairway.

Directions:
Answer these questions.

1. Would you travel a farther distance climbing a spiral stairway up three floors or climbing a ladder straight up three floors? _____

2. Which would take more force to climb—the stairway or the ladder? _____

3. When you climb a spiral stairway, you travel a greater _____, but you use less _____.

A screw is a special kind of inclined plane. A spiral stairway is also an inclined plane. Two or more inclined planes that are joined together to make a sharp edge or point form a wedge. A **wedge** is a special kind of inclined plane. A wedge is used to pierce or split things. A knife is a wedge. Can you name some other wedges?

Some special inclined planes are pictured below. Label each picture either a wedge or a screw.

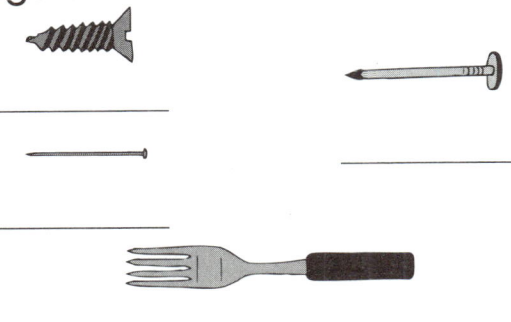

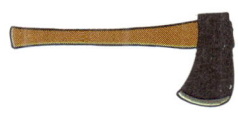

Find these special inclined planes in the puzzle to the right.

nail	stairway
fork	screw
pin	axe
knife	wedge

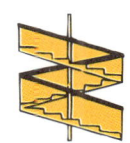

```
W G T P I N O K
E X W B D Z K N
D A Z K F E N I
G S C R E W P F
E A S K A X E E
J R F T U N K L
P A T O N A I L
S T A I R W A Y
V R T N O K O T
```

Published by Frank Schaffer Publications. Copyright protected.   **69**   Science: Grade 3

Simple Machines   Name_____

Simple + Simple = Compound

Many of the machines that you use each day are made up of two or more simple machines. What simple machines can you find in Mandy's bicycle? Find the gears, the wheel and axle machines and the levers. Machines that are made up of two or more simple machines are called **compound machines**.

Directions:

Look carefully at the compound machines pictured on this page. Find the simple machines that make up each compound machine. Label the simple machines you find.

Challenge
Find a compound machine in your home. Show someone in your family why it is a compound machine.

Simple Machines

Name _____

Work Savers

People use machines to help them with their work every day. Cars, trucks, sewing machines and bicycles have many moving parts. They are called **compound machines**.

Some machines have few or no moving parts. They are called **simple machines**. A hammer, a pulley and a ramp are all simple machines.

A simple machine makes work easier. It lets you do the work with less force, but you have to move the object a greater distance.

Directions: Look at the machines in the picture above. List each machine in the correct group.

Simple Machines	**Compound Machines**
_____	_____
_____	_____
_____	_____
_____	_____
_____	_____

Unscramble these mixed-up sentences.

1. work machines make easier. _____
_____

2. machines compound many have parts moving. _____
_____

3. force machines less do with you let work. _____
_____

4. machines no few or parts have moving simple. _____
_____

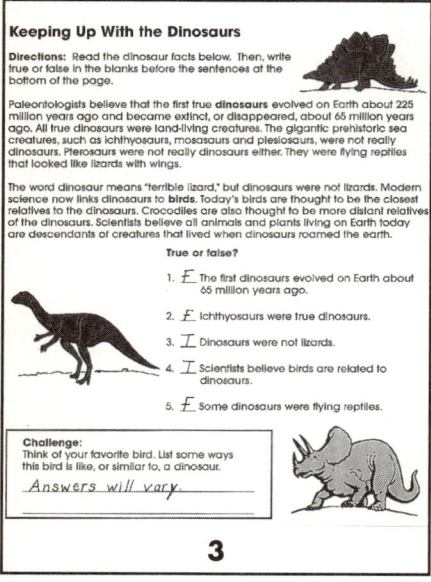

Keeping Up With the Dinosaurs

Directions: Read the dinosaur facts below. Then, write true or false in the blanks before the sentences at the bottom of the page.

Paleontologists believe that the first true **dinosaurs** evolved on Earth about 225 million years ago and became extinct, or disappeared, about 65 million years ago. All true dinosaurs were land-living creatures. The gigantic prehistoric sea creatures, such as ichthyosaurs, mosasaurs and plesiosaurs, were not really dinosaurs. Pterosaurs were not really dinosaurs either. They were flying reptiles that looked like lizards with wings.

The word dinosaur means "terrible lizard," but dinosaurs were not lizards. Modern science now links dinosaurs to **birds**. Today's birds are thought to be the closest relatives to the dinosaurs. Crocodiles are also thought to be more distant relatives of the dinosaurs. Scientists believe all animals and plants living on Earth today are descendants of creatures that lived when dinosaurs roamed the earth.

True or false?

1. _F_ The first dinosaurs evolved on Earth about 65 million years ago.
2. _F_ Ichthyosaurs were true dinosaurs.
3. _T_ Dinosaurs were not lizards.
4. _T_ Scientists believe birds are related to dinosaurs.
5. _F_ Some dinosaurs were flying reptiles.

Challenge:
Think of your favorite bird. List some ways this bird is like, or similar to, a dinosaur.
Answers will vary.

3

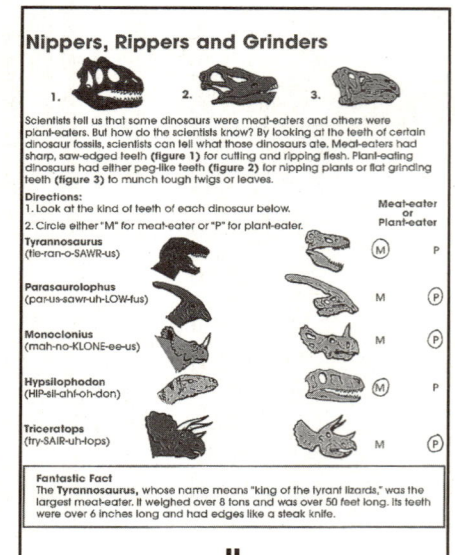

Nippers, Rippers and Grinders

Scientists tell us that some dinosaurs were meat-eaters and others were plant-eaters. But how do the scientists know? By looking at the teeth of certain dinosaur fossils, scientists can tell what those dinosaurs ate. Meat-eaters had sharp, saw-edged teeth **(figure 1)** for cutting and ripping flesh. Plant-eating dinosaurs had either peg-like teeth **(figure 2)** for nipping plants or flat grinding teeth **(figure 3)** to munch tough twigs or leaves.

Directions:
1. Look at the kind of teeth of each dinosaur below.
2. Circle either "M" for meat-eater or "P" for plant-eater.

	Meat-eater or Plant-eater
Tyrannosaurus (tie-ran-o-SAWR-us)	(M) P
Parasaurolophus (par-us-sawr-uh-LOW-fus)	M (P)
Monoclonius (mah-no-KLONE-ee-us)	M (P)
Hypsilophodon (HIP-sil-ahl-oh-don)	(M) P
Triceratops (try-SAIR-uh-tops)	M (P)

Fantastic Fact
The **Tyrannosaurus**, whose name means "king of the tyrant lizards," was the largest meat-eater. It weighed over 8 tons and was over 50 feet long. Its teeth were over 6 inches long and had edges like a steak knife.

4

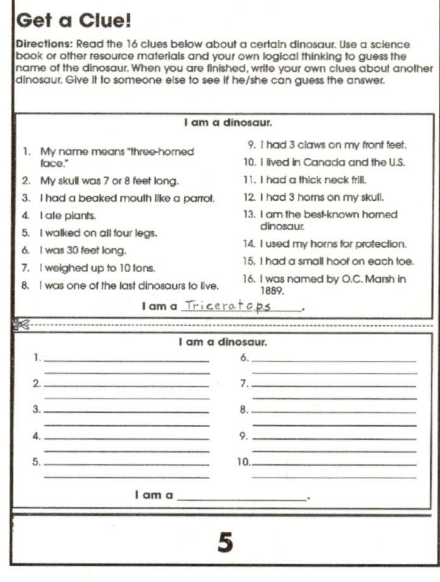

Get a Clue!

Directions: Read the 16 clues below about a certain dinosaur. Use a science book or other resource materials and your own logical thinking to guess the name of the dinosaur. When you are finished, write your own clues about another dinosaur. Give it to someone else to see if he/she can guess the answer.

I am a dinosaur.

1. My name means "three-horned face."
2. My skull was 7 or 8 feet long.
3. I had a beaked mouth like a parrot.
4. I ate plants.
5. I walked on all four legs.
6. I was 30 feet long.
7. I weighed up to 10 tons.
8. I was one of the last dinosaurs to live.
9. I had 3 claws on my front feet.
10. I lived in Canada and the U.S.
11. I had a thick neck frill.
12. I had 3 horns on my skull.
13. I am the best-known horned dinosaur.
14. I used my horns for protection.
15. I had a small hoof on each toe.
16. I was named by O.C. Marsh in 1889.

I am a _Triceratops_.

I am a dinosaur.

1. _____
2. _____
3. _____
4. _____
5. _____
6. _____
7. _____
8. _____
9. _____
10. _____

I am a _____.

5

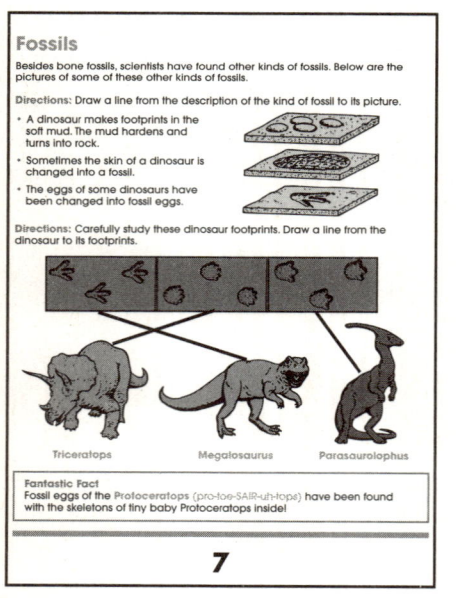

Fossils

Besides bone fossils, scientists have found other kinds of fossils. Below are the pictures of some of these other kinds of fossils.

Directions: Draw a line from the description of the kind of fossil to its picture.

- A dinosaur makes footprints in the soft mud. The mud hardens and turns into rock.
- Sometimes the skin of a dinosaur is changed into a fossil.
- The eggs of some dinosaurs have been changed into fossil eggs.

Directions: Carefully study these dinosaur footprints. Draw a line from the dinosaur to its footprints.

Triceratops   Megalosaurus   Parasaurolophus

Fantastic Fact
Fossil eggs of the **Protoceratops** (pro-toe-SAIR-uh-tops) have been found with the skeletons of tiny baby Protoceratops inside!

7

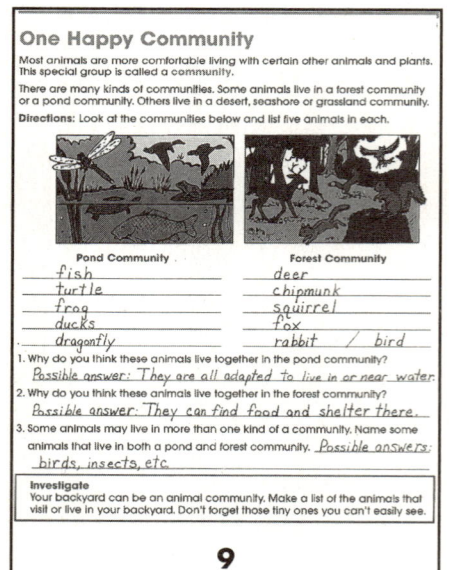

One Happy Community

Most animals are more comfortable living with certain other animals and plants. This special group is called a community.

There are many kinds of communities. Some animals live in a forest community or a pond community. Others live in a desert, seashore or grassland community.

Directions: Look at the communities below and list five animals in each.

Pond Community	Forest Community
fish	deer
turtle	chipmunk
frog	squirrel
ducks	fox
dragonfly	rabbit / bird

1. Why do you think these animals live together in the pond community?
Possible answer: They are all adapted to live in or near water.

2. Why do you think these animals live together in the forest community?
Possible answer: They can find food and shelter there.

3. Some animals may live in more than one kind of a community. Name some animals that live in both a pond and forest community. _Possible answers: birds, insects, etc._

Investigate
Your backyard can be an animal community. Make a list of the animals that visit or live in your backyard. Don't forget those tiny ones you can't easily see.

9

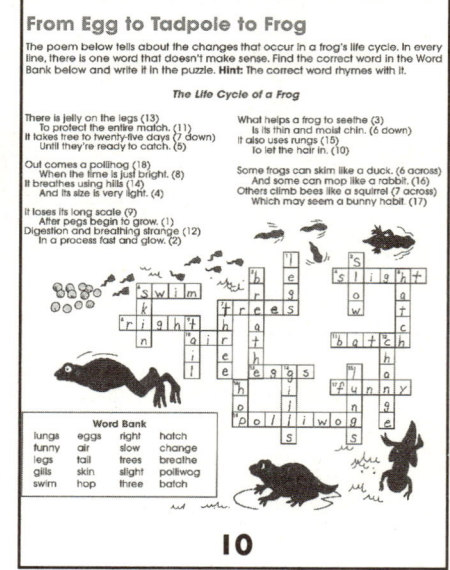

From Egg to Tadpole to Frog

The poem below tells about the changes that occur in a frog's life cycle. In every line, there is one word that doesn't make sense. Find the correct word in the Word Bank below and write it in the puzzle. **Hint:** The correct word rhymes with it.

The Life Cycle of a Frog

There is jelly on the legs (13)
To protect the entire match. (11)
It takes tree to twenty-five days (7 down)
Until they're ready to catch. (5)

Out comes a polliwog (18)
When the time is just bright. (8)
It breathes using hills (14)
And its size is very light. (4)

It loses its long scale (9)
After pegs begin to grow. (1)
Digestion and breathing strange (12)
In a process fast and glow. (2)

What helps a frog to seethe (3)
Is its thin and moist chin. (6 down)
It also uses rungs (15)
To let the hair in. (10)

Some frogs can skim like a duck. (6 across)
And some can mop like a rabbit. (16)
Others climb bees like a squirrel (7 across)
Which may seem a bunny habit. (17)

Word Bank
lungs   eggs   right   hatch
funny   air   slow   change
legs   tail   trees   breathe
gills   skin   slight   polliwog
swim   hop   three   batch

10

Toadly Froggin' Around

Directions:
Read the information about frogs and toads.
Then, write **true** or **false** in front of each statement at the bottom.

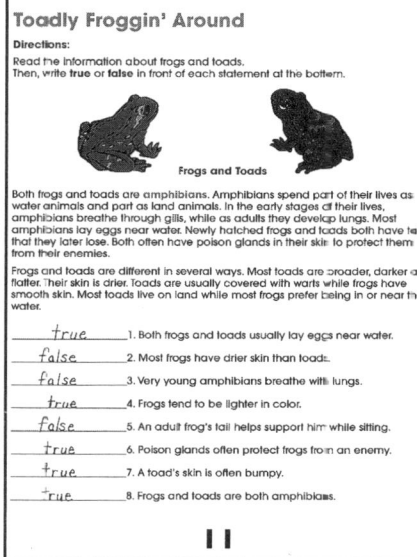
Frogs and Toads

Both frogs and toads are amphibians. Amphibians spend part of their lives as water animals and part as land animals. In the early stages of their lives, amphibians breathe through gills, while as adults they develop lungs. Most amphibians lay eggs near water. Newly hatched frogs and toads both have tails that they later lose. Both often have poison glands in their skin to protect them from their enemies.

Frogs and toads are different in several ways. Most toads are broader, darker and flatter. Their skin is drier. Toads are usually covered with warts while frogs have smooth skin. Most toads live on land while most frogs prefer being in or near the water.

true 1. Both frogs and toads usually lay eggs near water.
false 2. Most frogs have drier skin than toads.
false 3. Very young amphibians breathe with lungs.
true 4. Frogs tend to be lighter in color.
false 5. An adult frog's tail helps support him while sitting.
true 6. Poison glands often protect frogs from an enemy.
true 7. A toad's skin is often bumpy.
true 8. Frogs and toads are both amphibians.

11

Secret Code for Worm Lovers

Directions:
To decode the secret words, use the code below.

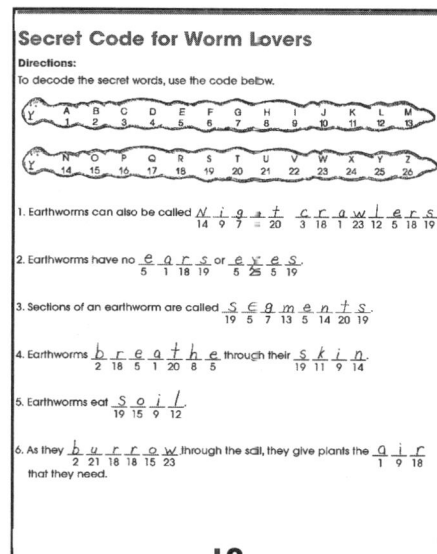

1. Earthworms can also be called _N i g h t_ _c r a w l e r s_
   14 9 7 8 20   3 18 1 23 12 5 18 19

2. Earthworms have no _e a r s_ or _e y e s_.
   5 1 18 19   5 25 5 19

3. Sections of an earthworm are called _s e g m e n t s_.
   19 5 7 13 5 14 20 19

4. Earthworms _b r e a t h e_ through their _s k i n_.
   2 18 5 1 20 8 5   19 11 9 14

5. Earthworms eat _s o i l_.
   19 15 9 12

6. As they _b u r r o w_ through the soil, they give plants the _a i r_
   2 21 18 18 15 23   1 9 18
   that they need.

12

Hibernation

Have you ever wondered why some animals hibernate? Some animals sleep all winter. This sleep is called hibernation.

Animals get their warmth and energy from food. Some animals cannot find enough food in the winter. They must eat large amounts of food in the autumn. Their bodies store this food as fat. Then, in winter, they hibernate. Their bodies live on the stored fat. Since their bodies need much less food during hibernation, they can stay alive without eating anymore food during the winter.

Some animals that hibernate are bats, chipmunks, bears, snakes and turtles.

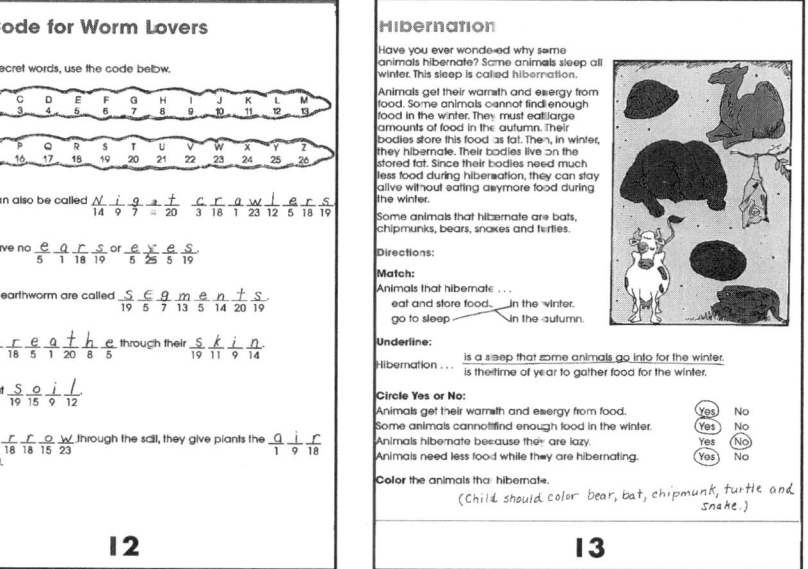

Directions:
Match:
Animals that hibernate . . .
   eat and store food. — In the winter.
   go to sleep — In the autumn.

Underline:
Hibernation . . . is a sleep that some animals go into for the winter.
   is the time of year to gather food for the winter.

Circle Yes or No:
Animals get their warmth and energy from food.   (Yes)   No
Some animals cannot find enough food in the winter.   (Yes)   No
Animals hibernate because they are lazy.   Yes   (No)
Animals need less food while they are hibernating.   (Yes)   No

Color the animals that hibernate.
(Child should color bear, bat, chipmunk, turtle and snake.)

13

Endangered Animals

You will never see a dodo bird or a saber-tooth tiger. These animals are gone forever. They are **extinct**.

The animals on this page are not extinct, but they are in danger of becoming extinct. They are **endangered**. There may not be enough of them to reproduce.

There are many reasons why some animals are endangered. The signs on this page give clues to three main reasons.

Look at the signs. What do you think the three reasons are? Write them below.

1. _Cutting down trees can eliminate shelter for wildlife._
2. _Hunters kill too many animals and disrupt food chains._
3. _Trash pollutes environments and kills animals._

Directions: Unscramble the names of these endangered animals.

dalb gleae   nereg teltur   lueb lawveh   brennit lofw
bald eagle   _green turtle_   _blue whale_   _timber wolf_

Investigate
There are more than 100 endangered animals in North America. Find the name of one that lives near your area. Make a poster to help people become aware of this animal and the danger it is in.

14

Going Places

Looking at a bird's feet can tell you a lot about how they are used. Look at the birds' feet below. Unscramble each bird's name. Write the bird's name by the sentence that best describes it.

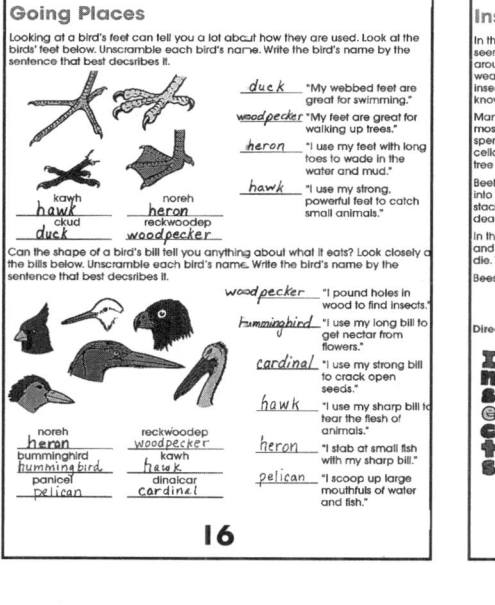

duck "My webbed feet are great for swimming."
woodpecker "My feet are great for walking up trees."
heron "I use my feet with long toes to wade in the water and mud."
hawk "I use my strong, powerful feet to catch small animals."

kawh   noreh   ckud   reckwoodep
hawk   _heron_   _duck_   _woodpecker_

Can the shape of a bird's bill tell you anything about what it eats? Look closely at the bills below. Unscramble each bird's name. Write the bird's name by the sentence that best describes it.

woodpecker "I pound holes in wood to find insects."
hummingbird "I use my long bill to get nectar from flowers."
cardinal "I use my strong bill to crack open seeds."
hawk "I use my sharp bill to tear the flesh of animals."
heron "I stab at small fish with my sharp bill."
pelican "I scoop up large mouthfuls of water and fish."

noreh   reckwoodep
heron   _woodpecker_
bumminghird   kawh
hummingbird   _hawk_
panicel   dinaicar
pelican   _cardinal_

16

Insects in Winter

In the summertime, insects can be seen buzzing and fluttering around us. But as winter's cold weather begins, suddenly the insects seem to disappear. Do you know where they go?

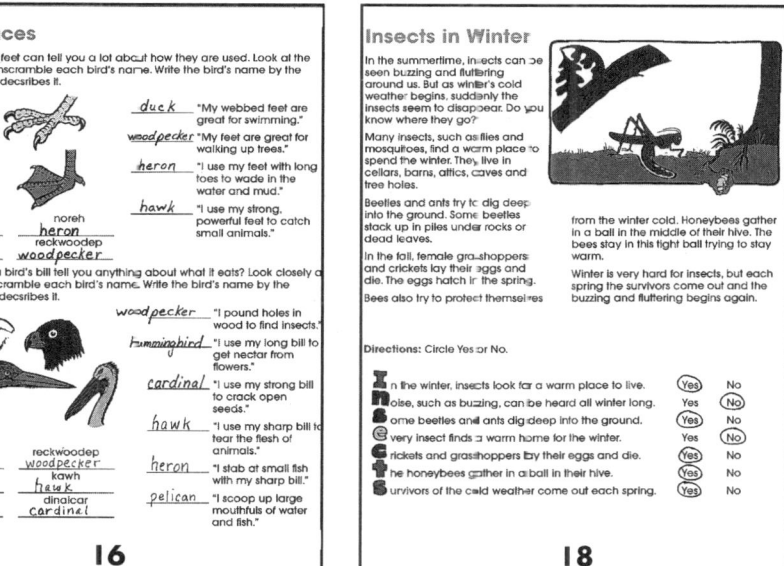

Many insects, such as flies and mosquitoes, find a warm place to spend the winter. They live in cellars, barns, attics, caves and tree holes.

Beetles and ants try to dig deep into the ground. Some beetles stack up in piles under rocks or dead leaves.

In the fall, female grasshoppers and crickets lay their eggs and die. The eggs hatch in the spring.

Bees also try to protect themselves from the winter cold. Honeybees gather in a ball in the middle of their hive. The bees stay in this tight ball trying to stay warm.

Winter is very hard for insects, but each spring the survivors come out and the buzzing and fluttering begins again.

Directions: Circle Yes or No.
In the winter, insects look for a warm place to live.   (Yes)   No
Noise, such as buzzing, can be heard all winter long.   Yes   (No)
Some beetles and ants dig deep into the ground.   (Yes)   No
Every insect finds a warm home for the winter.   Yes   (No)
Crickets and grasshoppers lay their eggs and die.   (Yes)   No
The honeybees gather in a ball in their hive.   (Yes)   No
Survivors of the cold weather come out each spring.   (Yes)   No

18

Body Building Blocks

Just like some houses are built with bricks, your body is built with cells. Every part of your body is made of cells.

Cells differ in **size** and **shape**, but they all have a few things in common. All cells have a **nucleus**. The **nucleus** is the center of the cell. It controls the cell's activities.

Cells can **divide** and become two cells exactly like the original cell.

Your body has many kinds of cells. Each kind has a special job. **Muscle** cells help you move. **Nerve** cells carry messages between your brain and other parts of your body. **Blood** cells carry **oxygen** to other cells in your body.

Directions:
Complete each sentence using the words in bold from above.

The _nucleus_ controls the cell's activities.
         3
Cells differ in _size_ and _shape_.
                2   1
One cell can _divide_ into two cells.
                 6
Muscle cells help you move.
   5
Blood cells carry _oxygen_ to other cells in your body.
                    4
Unscramble the numbered letters above to discover this amazing fact.

You began life as a _single_ cell
                     1 2 3 4 5 6

Fantastic Fact
People and most animals are made of billions or even trillions of cells. But some animals are made of only one cell. To find out more about these animals, look up **protozoans** in your library.

muscle cell
nucleus
nerve cell
blood cells

20

Framework

What gives you your **shape**? Like a house's frame, your body also has a frame. It is called your **skeleton**. Your skeleton is made of more than two hundred bones.

Your skeleton helps your body move. It does this by giving your **muscles** a place to attach. Your skeleton also **protects** the soft organs inside your body from injury.

Bones have a hard, outer layer made of **calcium**. Inside each bone is a soft, **spongy** layer that looks like a honeycomb. The hollow spaces in the honeycomb are filled with **marrow**. Every minute, millions of **blood** cells die. But you don't need to worry. The bone marrow works like a little factory, making new blood cells for you.

Directions:
Use the highlighted words above to finish the sentences below.

1. Your skeleton _protects_ your soft organs.
                      5
2. Bone _marrow_ makes new blood cells.
3. Inside the bone is a soft, _spongy_ layer.
                                    3
4. Millions of _blood_ cells die every minute.
                  4
5. The hard, outer layer of bone is made from _calcium_.
                                                    1
6. More than two hundred bones are in your _skeleton_.
                                                6
7. Your skeleton is a place for _muscles_ to attach.
                                       7
8. Your skeleton gives your body its _shape_.
                                          8

Challenge
What do you call a skeleton that won't get out of bed? Use the numbered letters above to find out.
lazy bones
 1 2 3   4 5 6 7 8

22

Breathing Tree

Did you know that you have a tree inside your chest? This tree has a special job. It takes air from your windpipe and spreads it all through your lungs. This tree is called your **bronchial tree**.

Air enters through your **nose**. It passes over the hairs inside your nose. This warms and cleanses the air. Then, it travels down your **windpipe** until it comes to your bronchial tree. The bronchial tree divides into two tubes. One tube sends air into your right **lung**. The other tube sends air into your left lung.

Inside the lungs, the air fills almost 300 million tiny, spongy **air sacs**. These air sacs give fresh **oxygen** to the blood. At the same time, they take away **carbon dioxide** from the blood. Carbon dioxide is the air that has already been used. When you exhale, the carbon dioxide flows up the bronchial tree and out of your mouth and nose. The nose, windpipe, bronchial tree, lungs and air sacs work as a team. The team is called the **respiratory system**.

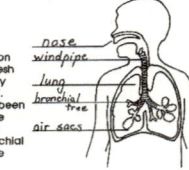
nose
windpipe
lung
bronchial tree
air sacs
Label the parts of the respiratory system.

Who am I?
Inhale these scrambled words. Exhale the answers to the riddles.

1. I warm and clean the air you breathe. SNOE _nose_
2. There are 300 million of me in your lungs. RAI SCAS _air sacs_
3. You breathe me out. RONBAC DOXEIDI _carbon dioxide_
4. I am your special tree. CHONRBALI REET _bronchial tree_
5. I am a long tube connecting your mouth to your lungs. DINWIPPE _windpipe_
6. I go through the air sacs and into the blood. YXONEG _oxygen_

Investigate
Smoking is harmful to your lungs. How can smoking affect breathing?

24

Your Body's Pipeline

Blood travels through three kinds of tubes. **Arteries** carry oxygen-rich blood from your heart to other parts of your body. Blood vessels, called **veins**, carry carbon dioxide-rich blood back to your heart. **Capillaries** are tiny vessels that connect arteries and veins. Capillaries take carbon dioxide from the cells and give the cells oxygen. Capillaries are fifty times thinner than a hair. They are so small that the blood cells must line up one at a time to travel through them.

Your heart, blood, arteries, veins and capillaries work as a team. This team is called your **circulatory system**.

Directions:
Name three kinds of blood vessels.
1. _arteries_
2. _veins_
3. _capillaries_

The picture shows your circulatory system.
1. Color the veins blue.
2. Color the arteries red.
3. Color the heart brown.

veins
arteries

Fantastic Fact
With every beat of your heart, blood starts a fantastic journey. Your blood travels through 60,000 miles of blood vessels to all the cells in your body.

25

Lub-Dub, Lub-Dub

Place your hand on the left side of your chest. Lub-dub, lub-dub. Did you feel it? This is your heart pumping oxygen-rich blood to all parts of your body.

Your heart is really two pumps. It is divided down the middle. Each half of the heart is divided into two chambers. The **right half** pumps blood filled with a waste called carbon dioxide gas into the lungs. The **left half** of the heart takes oxygen-rich blood from the lungs. It sends the oxygen-rich blood to the cells in your body.

What about lub-dub? These are the sounds made by the little "trap doors" called **valves**. The valves open and close to let the blood flow in and out of the heart.

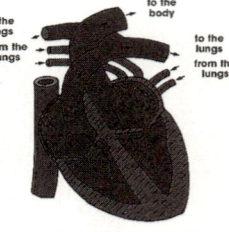
to the lungs
to the body
from the lungs
to the lungs
from the lungs

The arrows show the direction of blood flowing through the heart.

Directions:
Answer the questions below, using the information from above.

1. How many pumps does your heart have? _2_
2. Where does the right half pump its blood? _into the lungs_
3. Where does the left half pump its blood? _to the body's cells_
4. Which part of the heart makes the lub-dub sound? _valves_

26

Think Tank

Your brain has a very important job. It must keep your body working smoothly all day and night.

Your brain has three parts. The **cerebrum** is the largest part. It controls your body movement, such as running, walking, jumping, throwing a ball, holding a fork and other actions. It controls your five senses: hearing, smelling, tasting, seeing and touching. The cerebrum also controls your thinking and speaking.

The cerebrum is divided into two halves. The right half controls movements in the left side of your body. The left half controls movements in the right side of your body.

The part below the cerebrum is the **cerebellum**. The cerebellum makes sure that all of your muscles work together the way they should. It also helps you keep your balance.

The third and smallest part of the brain is the **brain stem**. The brain stem's job is extremely important. It controls breathing and the beating of your heart.

Directions: Label the three major parts of the brain.

cerebrum — controls your body movements
cerebellum — makes sure that all of your muscles work together
brain stem — controls breathing and the beating of your heart

1. Which part of the skeleton protects the brain from injury?
2. Give the common name and the scientific name.
   common name: _skull_   scientific name: _cranium_

Fantastic Fact
In order to function properly, the brain must have a constant supply of blood. The blood provides oxygen and other vitamins and nutrients needed by the brain to stay healthy.

27

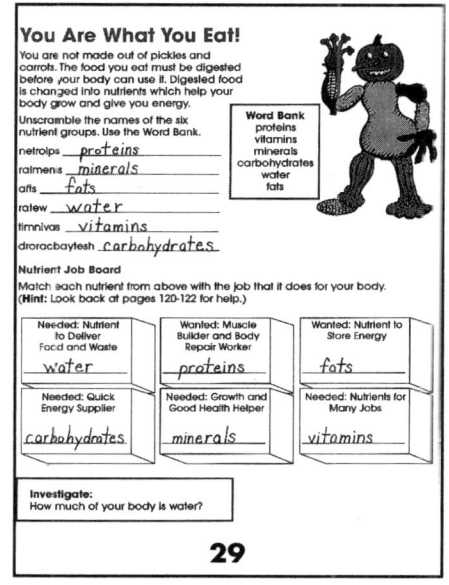
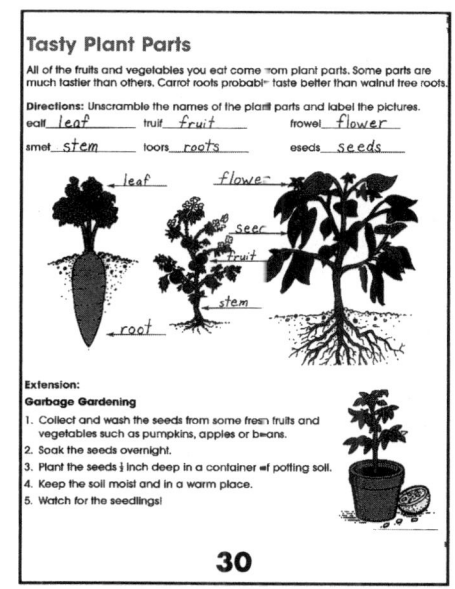
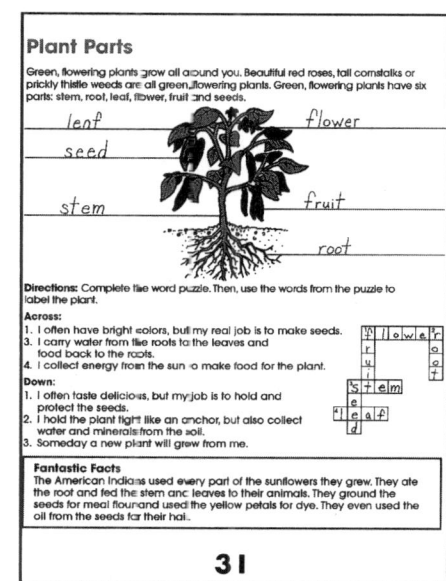
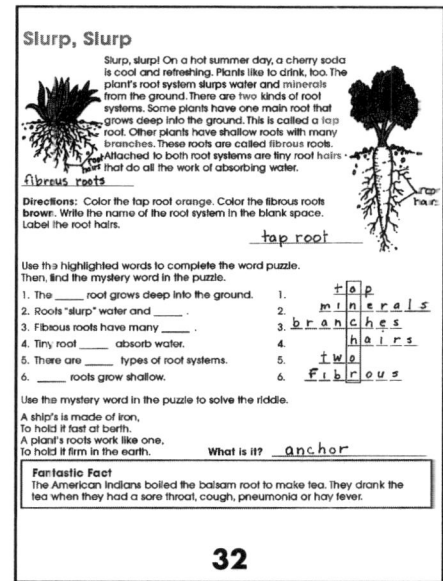
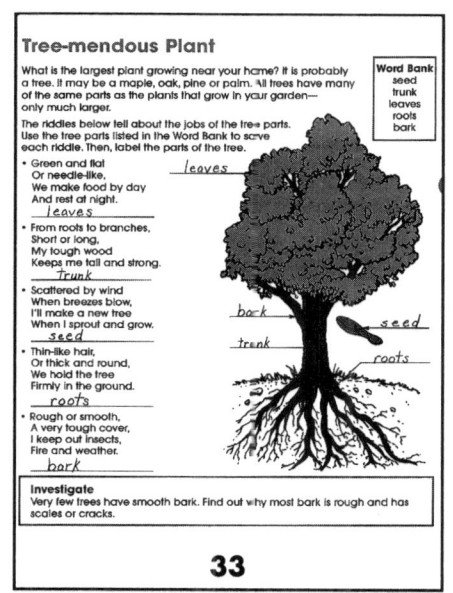
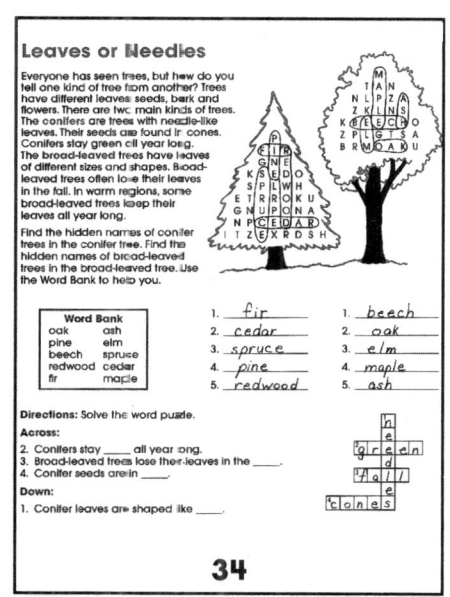

75

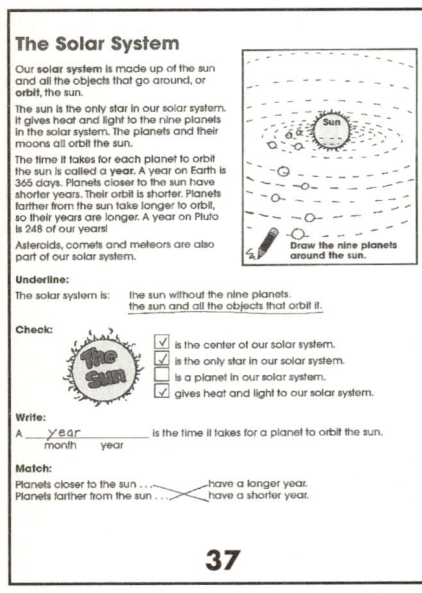
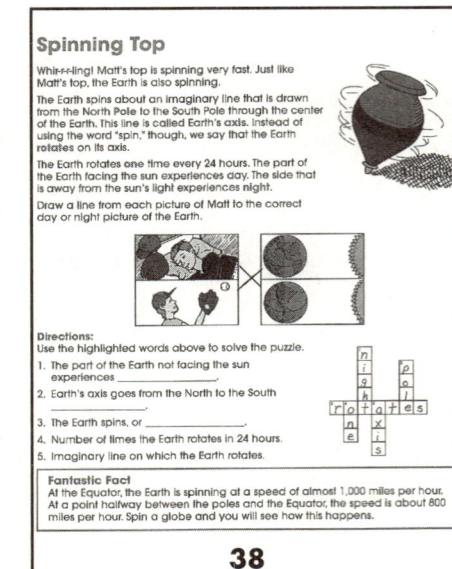
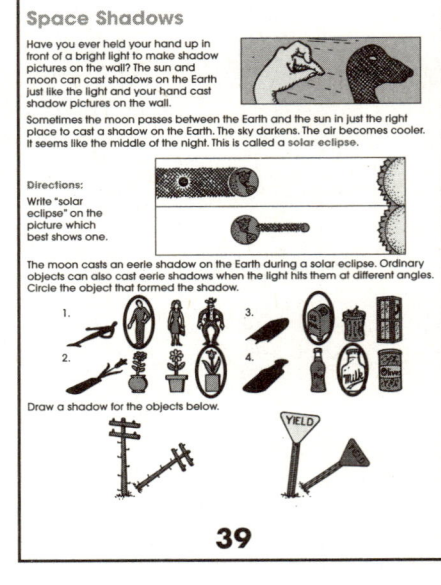
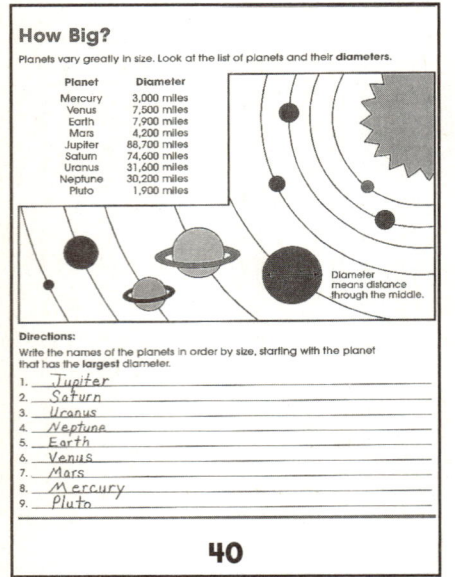
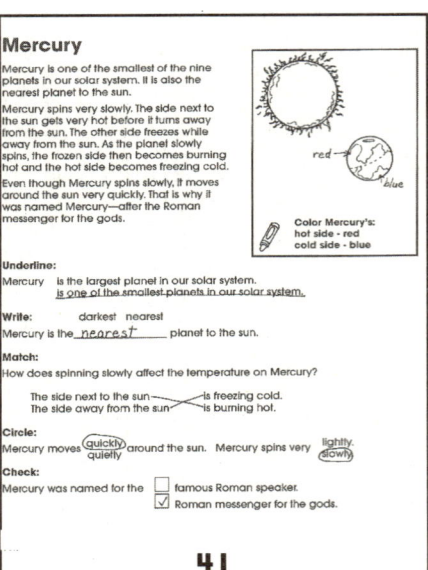
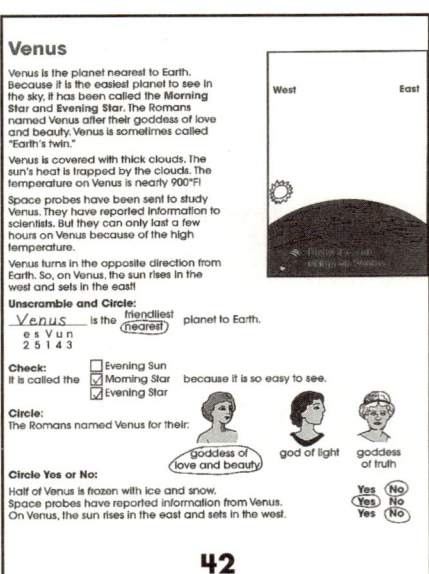

Jupiter

Jupiter is the largest planet in our solar system. It has sixteen moons. Jupiter is the second-brightest planet—only Venus is brighter.

Jupiter is bigger and heavier than all of the other planets together. It is covered with thick clouds. Many loose rocks and dust particles form a single, thin, flat ring around Jupiter.

One of the most fascinating things about Jupiter is its Great Red Spot. The Great Red Spot of Jupiter is a huge storm in the atmosphere. It looks like a red ball. This giant storm is larger than Earth! Every six days it goes completely around Jupiter.

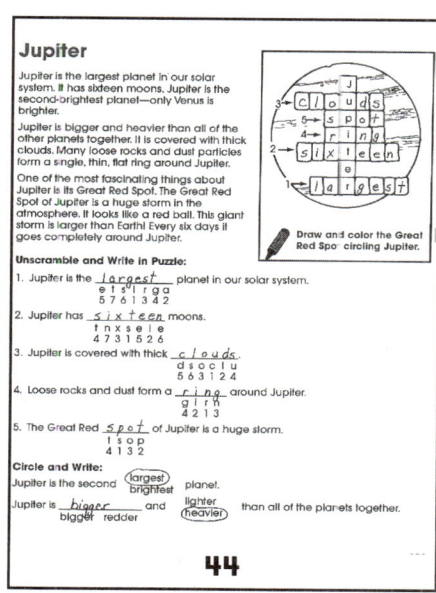

Draw and color the Great Red Spot circling Jupiter.

Unscramble and Write in Puzzle:
1. Jupiter is the _largest_ planet in our solar system.
2. Jupiter has _sixteen_ moons.
3. Jupiter is covered with thick _clouds_.
4. Loose rocks and dust form a _ring_ around Jupiter.
5. The Great Red _Spot_ of Jupiter is a huge storm.

Circle and Write:
Jupiter is the second (brightest) planet.
Jupiter is _bigger_ and (heavier) than all of the planets together.

44

Saturn

Saturn is probably most famous for its rings. These rings are made of billions of tiny pieces of ice and dust. Although these rings are very wide, they are very thin. If you look at the rings from the side, they are almost too thin to be seen.

Saturn is the second-largest planet in our solar system. It is so big that 758 Earths could fit inside it!

Saturn is covered by clouds. Strong, fast winds move the clouds quickly across the planet.

Saturn has 18 moons! Its largest moon is called Titan.

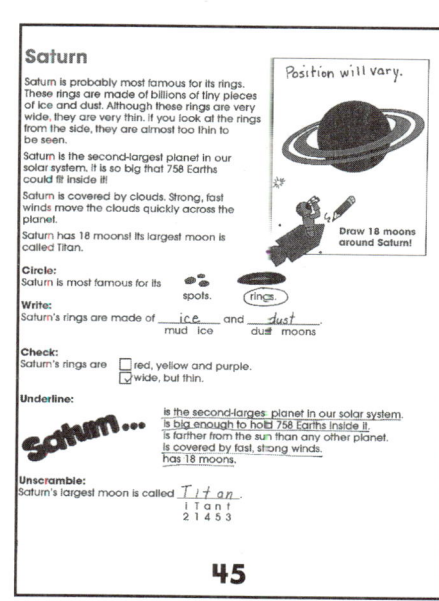

Position will vary. Draw 18 moons around Saturn!

Circle:
Saturn is most famous for its spots. (rings)

Write:
Saturn's rings are made of _ice_ and _dust_.

Check:
Saturn's rings are ☐ red, yellow and purple.
☑ wide, but thin.

Underline:
Saturn... is the second-largest planet in our solar system.
is big enough to hold 758 Earths inside it.
is farther from the sun than any other planet.
is covered by fast, strong winds.
has 18 moons.

Unscramble:
Saturn's largest moon is called _Titan_.

45

The Large Planets

Jupiter is about 88,836 miles at its equator. Named after the king of the Roman gods, it is the fifth-closest planet to the sun at about 483,600,000 miles away. Jupiter travels around the sun in an oval-shaped (elliptical) orbit. Jupiter also spins faster than any other planet and makes a complete rotation in about 9 hours and 55 minutes.

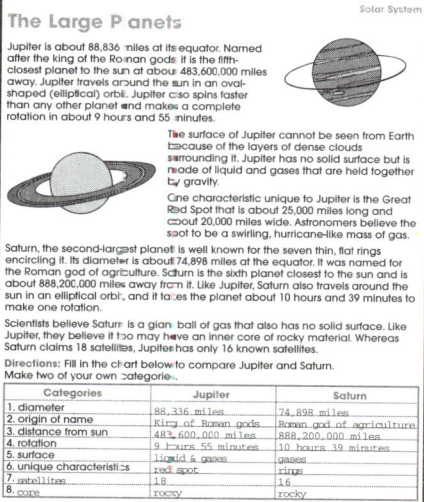

The surface of Jupiter cannot be seen from Earth because of the layers of dense clouds surrounding it. Jupiter has no solid surface but is made of liquid and gases that are held together by gravity.

One characteristic unique to Jupiter is the Great Red Spot that is about 25,000 miles long and about 20,000 miles wide. Astronomers believe the spot to be a swirling, hurricane-like mass of gas.

Saturn, the second-largest planet is well known for the seven thin, flat rings encircling it. Its diameter is about 74,898 miles at the equator. It was named for the Roman god of agriculture. Saturn is the sixth planet closest to the sun and is about 888,200,000 miles away from the sun. Like Jupiter, Saturn also travels around the sun in an elliptical orbit, and it takes the planet about 10 hours and 39 minutes to make one rotation.

Scientists believe Saturn is a giant ball of gas that also has no solid surface. Like Jupiter, they believe it too may have an inner core of rocky material. Whereas Saturn claims 18 satellites, Jupiter has only 16 known satellites.

Directions: Fill in the chart below to compare Jupiter and Saturn. Make two of your own categories.

Categories	Jupiter	Saturn
1. diameter	88,836 miles	74,898 miles
2. origin of name	King of Roman gods	Roman god of agriculture
3. distance from sun	483,600,000 miles	888,200,000 miles
4. rotation	9 hours 55 minutes	10 hours 39 minutes
5. surface	liquid & gases	gases
6. unique characteristics	red spot	rings
7. satellites	18	16
8. core	rocky	rocky

46

Uranus

Did you know that Uranus was first thought to be a comet? Many scientists studied the mystery comet. It was soon decided that Uranus was a planet. It was the first planet to be discovered through a telescope.

Scientists believe that Uranus is made of rock and metal with gas and ice surrounding it.

Even through a telescope, Uranus is not easy to see. That is because it is almost two billion miles from the sun that lights it. It takes 84 Earth years for Uranus to orbit the sun! Scientists know that Uranus has fifteen moons and is circled by ten thin rings. But there are still many mysteries about this faraway planet.

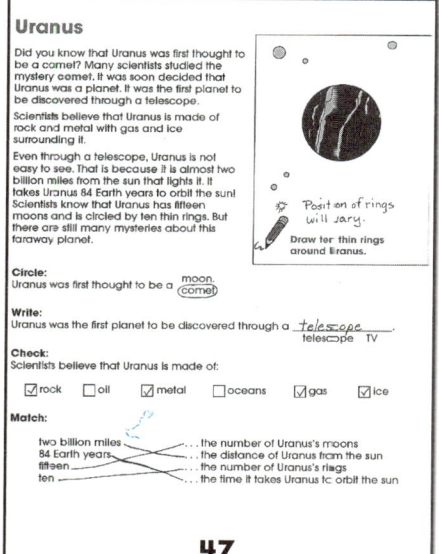

Position of rings will vary. Draw ten thin rings around Uranus.

Circle:
Uranus was first thought to be a moon. (comet)

Write:
Uranus was the first planet to be discovered through a _telescope_.

Check:
Scientists believe that Uranus is made of:
☑ rock ☐ oil ☑ metal ☐ oceans ☑ gas ☑ ice

Match:
two billion miles — the number of Uranus's moons
84 Earth years — the distance of Uranus from the sun
fifteen — the number of Uranus's rings
ten — the time it takes Uranus to orbit the sun

47

Neptune

Neptune is the eighth planet from the sun. It is difficult to see Neptune—even through a telescope. It is almost three billion miles from Earth.

Scientists believe that Neptune is much like Uranus—made of rock, iron, ice and gases.

Neptune has eight moons. Scientists believe that it may also have several rings.

Neptune is so far away from the sun that it takes 164 Earth years for it to orbit the sun just once!

Scientists still know very little about this cold and distant planet.

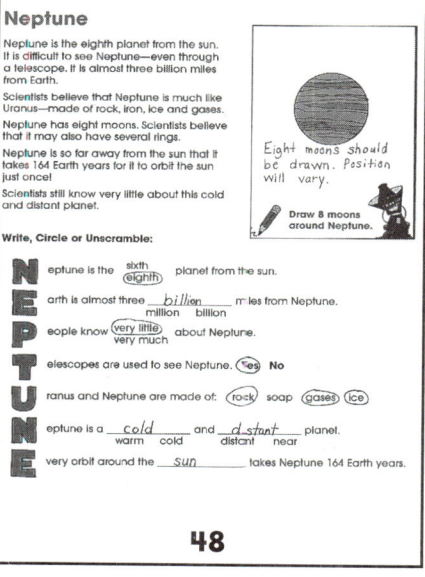

Eight moons should be drawn. Position will vary.

Draw 8 moons around Neptune.

Write, Circle or Unscramble:

Neptune is the (eighth) planet from the sun.
E**a**rth is almost three _billion_ miles from Neptune.
P**e**ople know (very little) about Neptune.
T**e**lescopes are used to see Neptune. (Yes) No
Uranus and Neptune are made of: (rock) soap (gases) (ice)
N**e**ptune is a _cold_ and _distant_ planet.
E**v**ery orbit around the _sun_ takes Neptune 164 Earth years.

48

The Twin Planets

1. Uranus and Neptune are similar in size, rotation time and temperature. Sometimes they are called twin planets. Uranus is about 1,786,400,000 miles from the sun. Neptune is about 2,798,800,000 miles from the sun. What is the difference between these two distances? _1,012,400,000 miles_

2. Neptune can complete a rotation in 18 to 20 hours. Uranus can make one in 16 to 18 hours. What is the average time it takes Neptune to complete a rotation? _19 hrs_ Uranus? _17 hrs_

3. Can you believe that it is about -353°F on Neptune, and about -357°F on Uranus? Brrr! That's cold! What is the temperature outside today in your town? _Answers will vary_. How much warmer is it in your town than on Neptune? _____ Uranus? _____

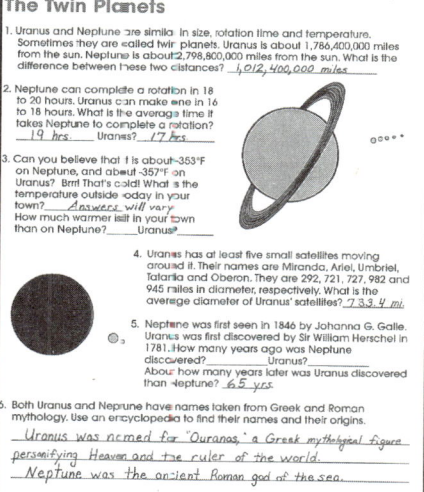

4. Uranus has at least five small satellites moving around it. Their names are Miranda, Ariel, Umbriel, Talaria and Oberon. They are 292, 721, 727, 982 and 945 miles in diameter, respectively. What is the average diameter of Uranus's satellites? _733.4 mi._

5. Neptune was first seen in 1846 by Johanna G. Galle. Uranus was first discovered by Sir William Herschel in 1781. How many years ago was Neptune discovered? _____ Uranus? _____
About how many years later was Uranus discovered than Neptune? _65 yrs_

6. Both Uranus and Neptune have names taken from Greek and Roman mythology. Use an encyclopedia to find their names and their origins.
Uranus was named for "Ouranos," a Greek mythological figure personifying Heaven and the ruler of the world.
Neptune was the ancient Roman god of the sea.

49

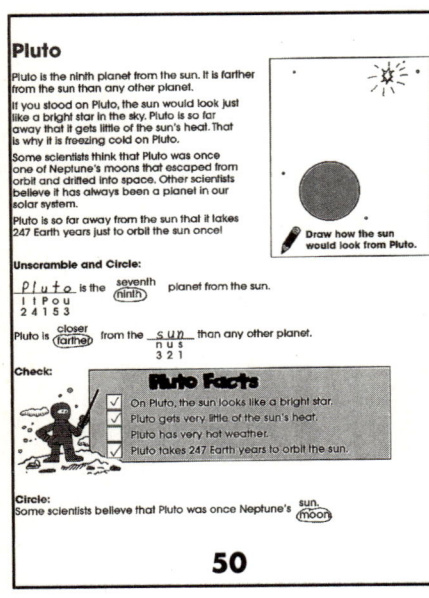
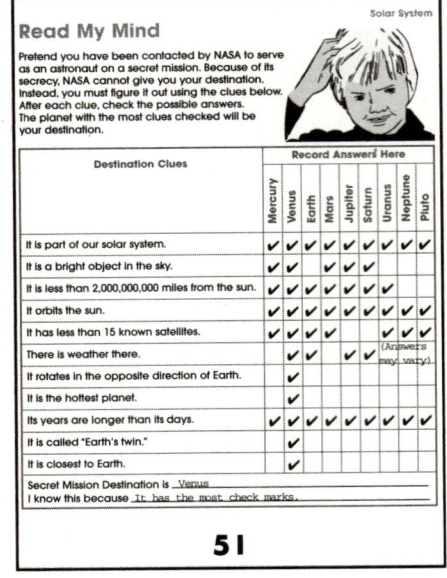
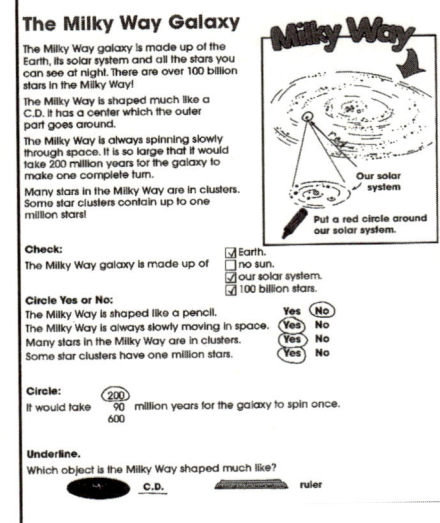
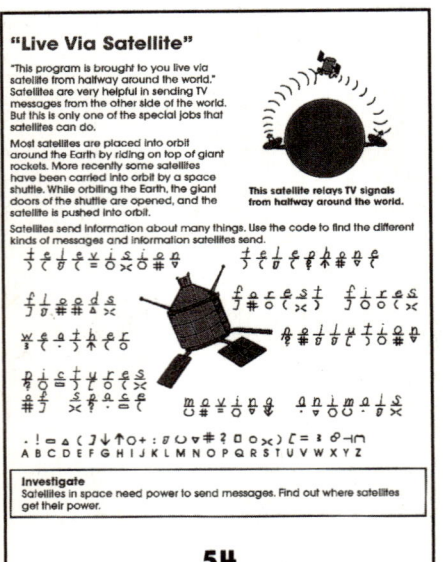
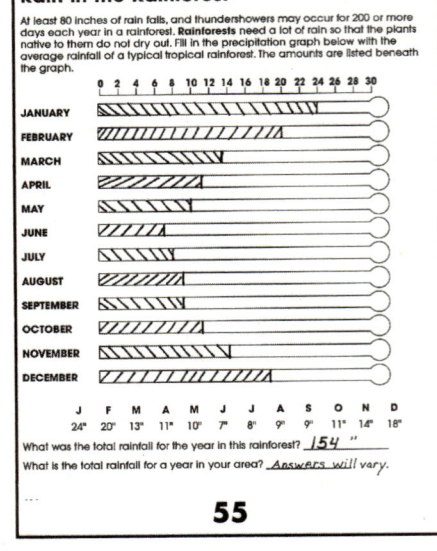
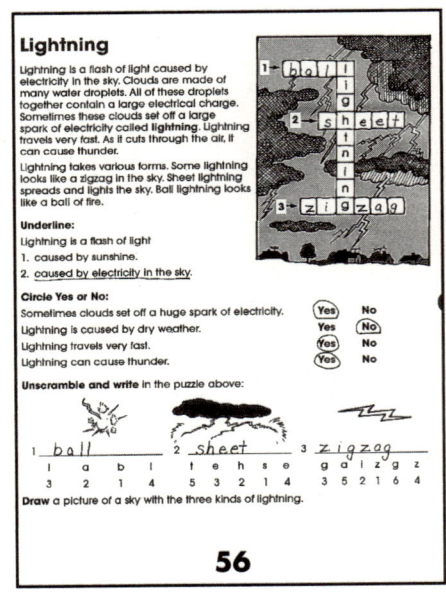

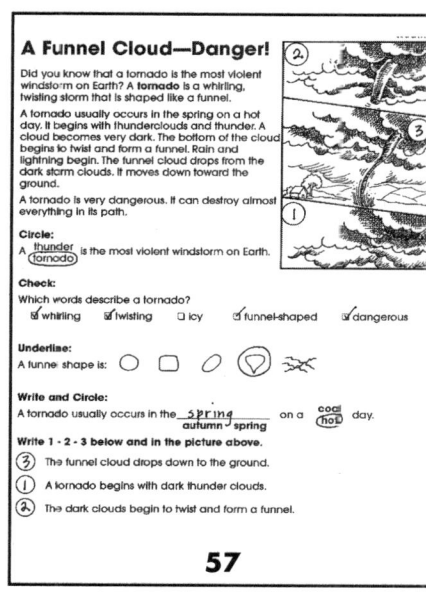
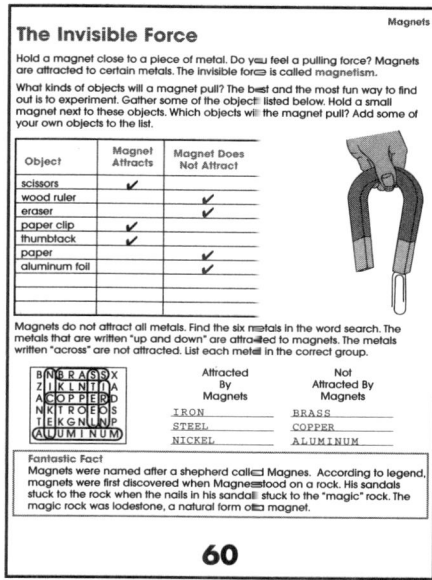
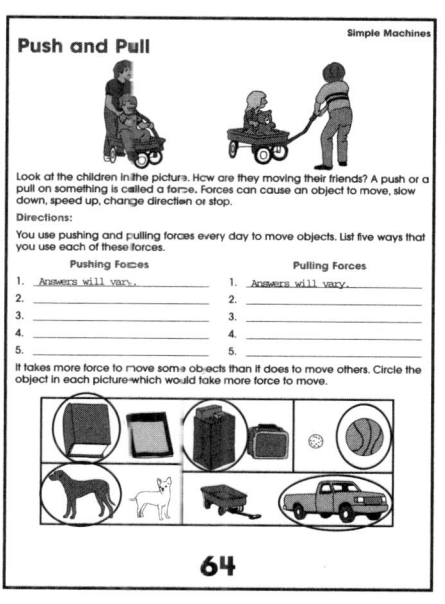
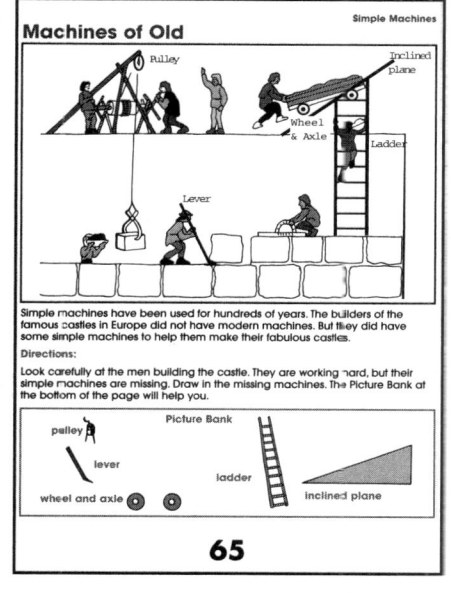
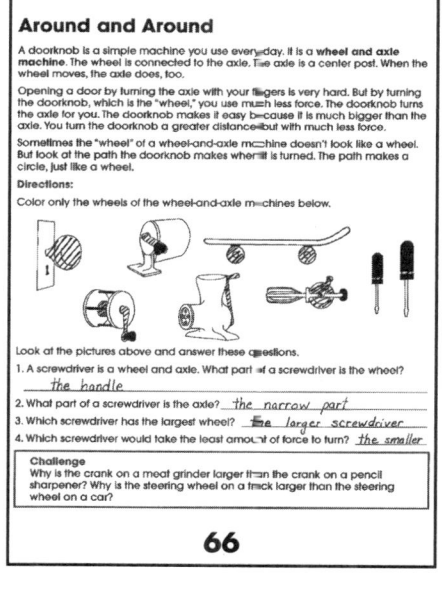
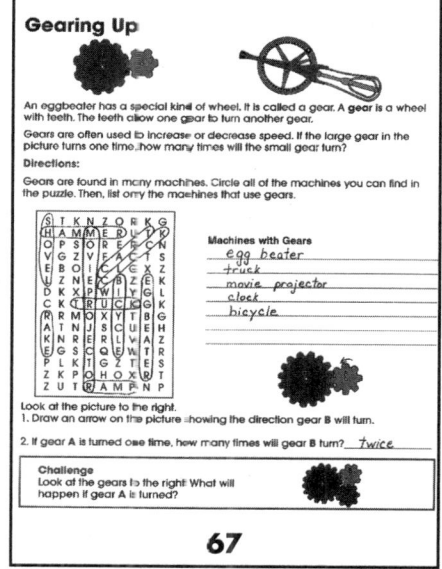

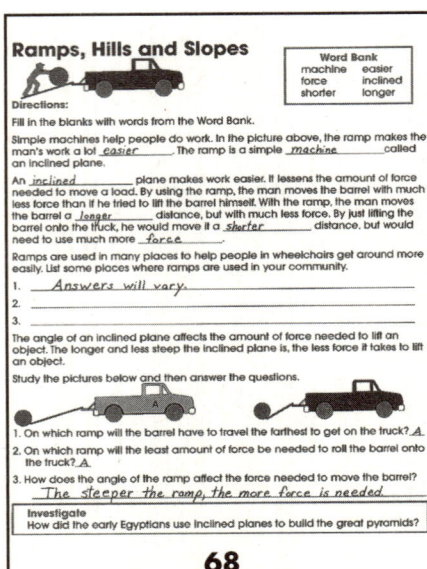

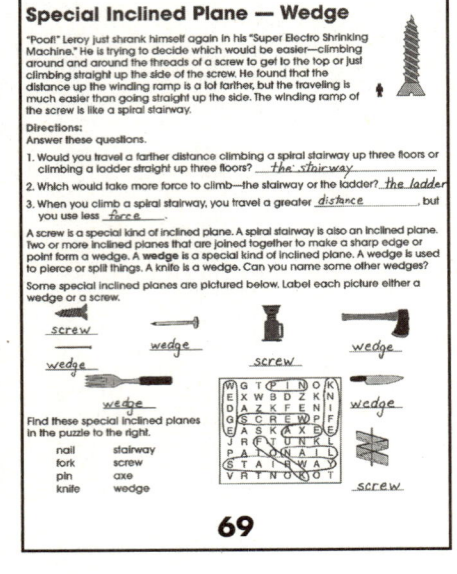

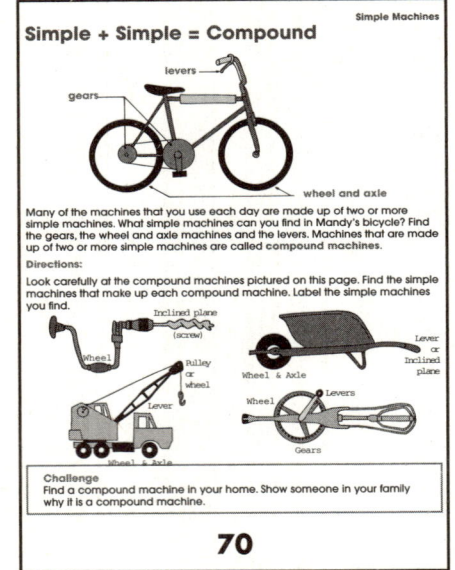

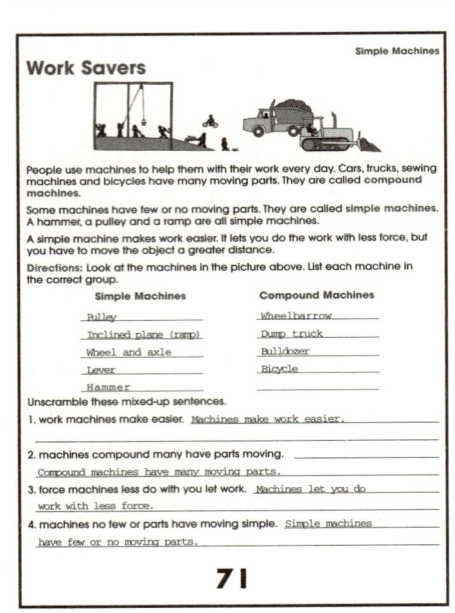